Living Fountains or Broken Cisterns

An Educational Problem for Protestants

"My people have committed two evils;
they have forsaken Me the fountain of living waters,
and hewed them out cisterns,
broken cisterns, that can hold no water."
Jeremiah 2:13

By E. A. Sutherland

Contents

Preface

THERE are few books which treat of the history of education, and fewer which attempt to show the part that the educational work has ever borne in the up building of nations. That religion is inseparably connected with, and upheld by, the system of education maintained by its advocates, has been recognized by many historians in a casual way; but, to the author's knowledge, no one has hitherto made this thought the subject of a volume.

In teaching the history of education and the growth of Protestantism, the close relationship ever existing between the latter and true methods of education led to a careful study of the educational system of the nations of the earth, especially of those nations which have exerted a lasting influence upon the world's history. The present volume is the result of that study.

D'Aubigné says that in the Reformation "the school was early placed beside the church; and these two great institutions, so powerful to regenerate the nations, were equally reanimated by it. It was by a close alliance with learning that the Reformation entered into the world."

True education, Protestantism, and republicanism form a threefold union which defies the powers of earth to overthrow; but today the Protestant churches are growing weak, and the boasted freedom of America's democracy is being exchanged for monarchical principles of government.

This weakness is rightly attributed by some to the want of proper education. The same cause of degeneracy would doubtless be assigned by many others, were effects traced to their source.

The author has attempted, by a generous use of historical quotations, to so arrange facts that the reader will see that the hope of Protestantism and the hope of republicanism lies in the proper education of the youth; and that this true education is found in the principles delivered by

Jehovah to his chosen people, the Jews; that it was afterward more fully demonstrated by the Master Teacher, Christ; that the Reformation witnessed a revival of these principles; and that Protestants today, if true to their faith, will educate their children in accordance with these same principles.

Due credit is given to the authors quoted, a list of whose names appears at the end of the volume. A complete index renders this work easy of reference.

E.A.S.

Chapter I
Introductory:
God the Source of Wisdom

SURELY there is a vein for the silver, and a place for gold where they refine it. Iron is taken out of the earth, and brass is molten out of the stone....

"As for the earth, out of it cometh bread; and under it is turned up as it were fire. The stones of it are the place of sapphires; and it hath dust of gold.

"There is a path which no fowl knoweth, and which the vulture's eye hath not seen. The lion's whelps have not trodden it, nor the fierce lion passed by it....

"*But where shall wisdom be found? And where is the place of understanding?* Man knoweth not the price thereof; neither is it found in the land of the living. The depth saith, It is not in me; and the sea saith, It is not with me. *It cannot be gotten for gold*, neither shall silver be weighed for the price thereof....The gold and the crystal cannot equal it; and the exchange of it shall not be for jewels of fine gold.... *Whence then cometh wisdom?* And where is the place of understanding?...*God understandeth the way thereof, and He knoweth the place thereof.*"[1]

Man sometimes feels that *he* understands the way of wisdom, and boasts that he *knows* the place thereof. He may indeed understand it in a measure, and he may ascertain its abiding place; but that knowledge comes in one way, and only one. He who understandeth the way thereof and knoweth the place thereof, opens a channel which connects earth with that fountain of life.

In the creation of the universe that wisdom was manifested. "When He made a decree for the *rain*, and a way for the *lightning of the thunder*; then did He see it, and declare it; He prepared it, yea, and searched it out." Written on the face of creation is the wisdom of the Eternal. "And unto man He said, Behold, the fear of the Lord, that is wisdom; and to depart from evil is understanding." In other words, when man lives in harmony with God—that is, when physically he acts in accordance with the laws of the universe; when mentally his thoughts are those of the Father; and when spiritually his soul responds to the drawing power of love, that power which controls creation—then has he entered the royal road which leads direct to wisdom.

Where is the wise? There is implanted in each human heart a longing to come in touch with wisdom. God, by the abundance of life, is as a great magnet, drawing humanity to Himself. So close is the union that in Christ are hidden all the treasures of wisdom and knowledge. In one man—a man made of flesh and blood like all men now living—there dwelt the spirit of wisdom. More than this, in Him are "hid all the treasures of wisdom"; and hence the life of Immanuel stands a constant witness that the wisdom of the ages is accessible to man. And the record adds, "Ye are complete in Him."

This wisdom brings eternal life; for in Him are "hid all the treasures of wisdom," "and ye are complete in Him." "This is life eternal, that they might know Thee the only true God."

Christ, at Jacob's well, explained to the woman of Samaria, and through her to you and me, the means of gaining wisdom. The well of living water, from the depths of which the patriarch had drawn for himself, his children, and his cattle, and which he bequeathed as a rich legacy to generations following, who drank, and blessed his name, symbolized worldly wisdom. Men today mistake this for that wisdom described in Job, of which God understandeth the way and knoweth the place. Christ spoke of this latter when He said, "If thou knewest the gift of God, and who it is that saith to thee, Give me to drink; thou wouldst have asked of

Him, and He would have given thee *living water.*" "If any man thirst, let him come unto Me, and drink."

Why, then, if wisdom may be had for the asking, if that spiritual drink may be had for the taking, are not all filled? The fountain flows free; why are not all satisfied? Only one reason can be given: men in their search accept falsehood in place of truth. This blunts their sensibilities, until the false seems true and the true false.

"Where is the wise?...hath not God made foolish the wisdom of this world?" "Howbeit we speak wisdom among the perfect (full-grown); yet a wisdom not of this world, nor of the rulers of this age which are coming to naught: but we speak God's wisdom in a mystery, even the wisdom that hath been hidden, which none of the rulers of this world knoweth."[2]

There is, then, a distinction between the wisdom of God and that of this world. How, then, can we attain unto the higher life—to the real, the true wisdom? There are things which eye hath not seen nor ear heard, which eyes should see and ears hear, and these "God hath revealed unto us by His Spirit: for the Spirit searcheth all things, yea, the deep things of God."

To man, then, if born of the Spirit, is given a spiritual eyesight which pierces infinitude, and enables the soul to commune with the Author of all things. No wonder the realization of such possibilities within himself led the psalmist to exclaim, "Such knowledge is too wonderful for me; it is high, I cannot attain unto it." And Paul himself exclaimed, "O the depth of the riches both of the *wisdom* and *knowledge* of God!...For who hath known the mind of the Lord?" "The things of God knoweth no man, but the Spirit of God." And "we have received, not the spirit of the world, but the Spirit which is of God; that we might know the things that are freely given to us of God." Hence to us is given the power to commune with Him and to search into the mysteries of the otherwise unfathomable.

Dealing with wisdom is education. If it be the wisdom

of the world, then it is *worldly education*; if, on the other hand, it is a search for the wisdom of God, it is Christian education.

Over these two questions the controversy between good and evil is waging. The final triumph of truth will place the advocates of Christian education in the kingdom of God. "God is a Spirit: and they that worship Him must worship in spirit and in truth."

That education which links man with God, the source of wisdom, and the author and finisher of our faith, is a spiritual education, and prepares the heart for that kingdom which is within.

Chapter II
The Heavenly School

GOD'S throne, the center around which circled the worlds which had gone forth from the hand of the Creator, was the school of the universe. The Upholder of the worlds was Himself the great Teacher, and His character, love, was the theme of contemplation. Every lesson was a manifestation of His power. To illustrate the workings of the laws of His nature, this Teacher had but to speak, and before the attentive multitudes there stood the living thing. "He spake, and it was; He commanded, and it stood fast."[3]

Angels, and the beings of other worlds in countless numbers, were the students. The course was to extend through eternity; observations were carried on through limitless space, and included everything from the smallest to the mightiest force, from the formation of the dewdrop to the building of the worlds and the growth of the mind. To finish the course, if such an expression is permissible, meant to reach the perfection of the Creator Himself.

To the angelic host was given a work. The inhabitants of worlds were on probation. It was the joy of angels to minister to and teach other creatures of the universe. The law of love was everywhere written; it was the constant study of the heavenly beings. Each thought of God was taken by them; and as they saw the workings of His plans, they fell before the King of kings, crying, "Holy, holy, holy." Eternity was all too short to reveal His love.

The Father and Son were often in council. Wrapped together in that glory, the universe awaited the expression of Their one will. As one of the covering cherubim, Lucifer stood the first in power and majesty of all the angelic host. His eye beheld, his ear heard, he knew of all except the deep counsels which the Father, from all eternity, had purposed in the Son. "Christ the Word, the only begotten of God, was one with the eternal Father—one in nature, in character, in purpose—the only being that could enter into all the counsels and purposes of God....The Father Wrought by His Son in the creation of all heavenly beings. 'By Him were all things created,...whether they be thrones, or dominions, or principalities, or powers. All things were created by Him, and for Him.' Angels are God's ministers, radiant with the light ever flowing from His presence, and speeding on rapid wing to execute His will. But the Son, the anointed of God, the 'express image of His person,' the 'brightness of his glory,' 'upholding all things by the word of His power,' holds supremacy over them all." Lucifer, "son of the morning," who "sealest up the sum, full of wisdom, and perfect in beauty,...every precious stone was thy covering." "Thou art the anointed cherub that covereth; I have set thee so; thou wast upon the holy mountain of God; thou hast walked up and down in the midst of the stones of fire."⁴ He who had hovered over the throne of God, who had stood on the mount of the congregation in the sides of the north, and walked up and down among those living stones, each flashing with electric brightness the glory of reflected light, looked upon the council, and envied the position of the Son.

Hitherto, all eyes had turned instinctively toward the center of light. A cloud, the first one known, darkened the glory of the covering cherub. Turning his eyes inward, he reasoned that he was wronged. Had not he, Lucifer, been the bearer of light and joy to worlds beyond? Why should not his might be recognized? "Thou wast perfect in thy ways from the day that thou wast created till iniquity was found in thee." "Thine heart was lifted up because of thy beauty, thou hast corrupted thy wisdom by reason of thy brightness."⁵ "Thou hast said in thine heart, I will ascend into heaven, I will exalt my throne above the stars of God: I will sit also upon the mount of the congregation, in the sides of the north: I will ascend above the heights of the clouds: I will be like the Most High."[6]

While Lucifer thus reasoned, Christ, wrapped within the glory of the Father, was offering His life for the world at its creation. Sin had not yet entered, the world was not yet created; but as the plans were laid, the Son had said, "Should sin enter, I am, from this time, one with those We now create, and their fall will mean My life on earth. Never has My heart gone out for any creation as I put it into this. Man, in his earthly home, shall have the highest expression of Our love, and for him My love demands that I lay My life beside his in his very creation." O wondrous gift! O unselfish love! How could that covering cherub, at the moment when the Son of God laid down His life, plan on his own exaltation? Sorrow, the first sorrow that was ever known, filled heaven. The angel choir was silent; the living stones withheld their shining. The stillness was felt throughout the universe.

An offer was made to return, but pride now closed the channel. Pity and admiration for the leader of the hosts led many to feel that God was unjustly severe. The universe was off trial. "Satan and his sympathizers were striving to reform the government of God. They wished to look into His unsearchable wisdom, and ascertain His purpose in exalting Jesus, and endowing Him with such unlimited power and command." Those who before, inspired by love, took God at His word, and found their highest pleasure in watching the revealings of His love, now put their own minds in place of God's word, and reasoned that all was wrong. The unfoldings of His love, which had meant their very life, now looked but darkness and despair. God's wisdom, darkened by placing self between the throne and them, became foolishness. "All the heavenly host were summoned to appear before the Father to have each case decided." "About the throne gathered the holy angels, a vast, unnumbered throng—'ten thousand times ten thousand, and thousands of thousands,'—the most exalted angels, as ministers and subjects, rejoicing in the light that fell upon them from the presence of the Deity."

The principles of God's government were now laid bare: it was nothing but a great, broad system of educational development, and angelic hosts then and there decided whether faith in His word would be the standard of their obedience, or whether finite reason would bear sway. Even Satan himself was almost won, as the notes of praise resounded through the domes of heaven; but again, pride ruled. Here was born the rival system—supreme selfishness facing the utter self-forgetfulness of Christ, reason over against faith. After long pleadings, and amidst deep mourning, heaven's portals opened to close forever upon the one who, with his followers, turned from light into the darkness of despair.

A new era was ushered in; a controversy was begun. High heaven, with its eternal principles of love, life, progress, was challenged by a subtle foe, the father of lies. Deep as is the misery attending the step, yet coexistent with the downward move was formulated the plan which, after the lapse of ages, will prove in a greater degree, and manifest eternally the truth, that "God is love." The pathway is the way of the cross. It is a retracing of the mental degradation occasioned by the fall, but the process is according to the law of the school of heaven—"according to your faith." If ye believe, all things are possible.

Chapter III
The Edenic School

HE spake, and it was; He commanded, and it stood fast."[7] Forth from the throne of the Infinite passed the decree, and life flashing out into space, a world stood forth. Myriads of other worlds, held in their orbits by the ceaseless power of love, made their circuit about the throne of God. But one space in the universe had been reserved for the highest expression of His love, where was to be manifested the depths of this divine attribute. "And the earth was waste and void; and darkness was upon the face of the deep."[8]

But even into the darkness His presence penetrated; and as "the Spirit of God was brooding upon the waters," He said, "Let there be light," and darkness scattered before the word. The light, reflective of His own being, pleased Him; and He willed that it should be ever present, accompanying every form of life. The first day's work was done—a day such as the future man would know, and which, even in his fallen state, would measure off his years.

The second day heard the mandate for the water to separate; and a third gathered the waters into seas, with the dry land appearing. And then "God said, Let the earth put forth grass,"—the lowly blade covering the earth's nakedness with a robe of living green, itself so humble, yet a part of His life; for his life-breath formed it, and it partook of that life. Then came the herbs and lofty trees, each bearing seed—self-productive—for *life is* reproductive; and as the living coal kindles a sacred fire, so each tree bore within itself the power to reproduce its kind. "And God saw that it was good." Then, that His own light might ever be the cause of growth, He placed luminaries in the heavens, each being the reflection of His own countenance. By this should life be sustained.

Into the moving waters passed the power of life. "God said, Let the waters swarm with swarms of living creatures, and let fowl fly above the earth in the open firmament of heaven."[9] At His word an abundance of life filled earth and sky and sea. Every drop of water sustained life; every square inch of air supported its myriads. And, from the mighty leviathan that sported in the waters to the mote that floated in the air, all life proclaimed the love of God; and the Creator, viewing with satisfaction the work of His hand, pronounced each form of life perfect in its sphere. Each held within its own body the breath of life; each in its every movement sang hallelujahs to the Maker of the heavens and the earth.

But the work was not yet complete. A mind controlled the universe; and its powers could be appreciated, its heart-love returned in the fullest sense, only by mind—by beings made in the image of God Himself. And so "God said, Let Us make man in Our image, after Our likeness." He can then hold dominion over the lower orders of creation, and standing to them as We do to the universe, all nature will see Our power in him. "So, God created man in His own image, in the image of God created He him; male and female created He them."[10]

As if the moment of supreme endeavor had been reached even by God, He molded the form of clay—one, only one—in the image of Himself. He breathed into its nostrils His own breath—that breath which, vocalized, moved the worlds; before which angels bowed in adoration. That all-pervading element of life surged through the mighty frame, the organs performed their functions, the brain worked; the man Adam stood forth, strong and perfect; and instead of the piercing wail which now announces the beginning of a new life, his lips parted, and a song of praise ascended to the Creator.

Standing by his side was his Elder Brother, Christ, the King of heaven. Adam felt the thrill of unity and harmony; and while for a "little time inferior;" yet within him lay the possibilities of attaining greater heights than angels held. He was to be the companion of God, the perfect reflection of His light and glory; there was no thought of God that might not have access to the brain of man. The universe spread out in panoramic view before him. The earth, newborn, presented untold beauties. By his side stood his companion, the other half of his own nature, the two forming a perfect whole. The harmony of thought brought strength and life; and, as a result of this unity, new beings like themselves would be brought into existence, until the earth was peopled.

God planted a garden eastward in Eden, and from the beauties of the earth chose the most beautiful spot for the home of the new pair. In the midst of the garden stood the tree of life, the fruit of which afforded man a perfect physical food. Beneath its spreading branches God Himself visited them, and, talking with them face to face, revealed to them the way of immortality. As they ate of the fruit of the tree of life, and found every physical want supplied, they were constantly reminded of the need of the spiritual meat which was gained by open converse with the Light from heaven. The glory of God surrounded the tree, and enwrapped in this halo, Adam and Eve spent much time in communing with the heavenly visitors. According to the divine system of teaching, they were here to study the laws of God and learn of His character. They "were not only His children, but students receiving instruction from the all-wise Creator." Angels, beholding the wonders of the new creation, delighted to fly earthward; and two from the heavenly host, by special appointment, became the instructors of the holy ones. "They were full of vigor imparted by the tree of life, and their intellectual power was but little less than that of the angels. The mysteries of the visible universe—the wondrous works of Him who is perfect in knowledge—afforded them an exhaustless source of instruction and delight. The laws and operations of nature, which have engaged men's study for six thousand years, were opened to their minds by the infinite Framer and Upholder of the universe.

"They held converse with leaf and flower and tree, gathering from each the secrets of its life. With every living creature, from the mighty leviathan that playeth among the waters to the insect mote that floats in the sunbeam, Adam was familiar. He had given to each its name, and he was acquainted with the nature and habits of all. God's glory in the heavens, the innumerable worlds in their orderly revolutions, the balancing of the clouds, the mysteries of light and sound, of day and night—all were open to the study of our first parents. On every leaf of the forest or stone of the mountains, in every shining star, in earth and air and sky, God's name was written. The order and harmony of creation spoke to them of infinite wisdom and power. They were ever discovering some attraction that filled their hearts with deeper love, and called forth fresh expressions of gratitude."

As new beauties came to their attention, they were filled with wonder. Each visit of the heavenly teachers elicited from the earthly students scores of questions which it was the delight of the angels to answer; and they in turn opened to the minds of Adam and Eve principles of living truth which sent them forth to their daily tasks of pleasure full of wondering curiosity, ready to use every God-given sense to discover illustrations of the wisdom of heaven. "As long as they remained loyal to the divine law, their capacity to know, to enjoy, and to love would continually increase. They would be constantly gaining new treasures of knowledge, discovering fresh springs of happiness, and obtaining clearer and yet clearer conceptions of the immeasurable, unfailing love of God." The divine method of teaching is here of revealed—God's way of dealing with minds which are loyal to Him. The governing laws of the universe were expounded. Man, as if looking into a picture, found in earth, sky, and sea, in the animate and inanimate world, the exemplification of those laws. He believed, and with a heavenly light, which is the reward of faith, he approached each new subject of investigation. Divine truths unfolded continually. Life, power, happiness—these subjects grew with his growth.

The angels stimulated the desire to question, and again led their students to search for answers to their own questions. At his work of dressing the garden, Adam learned truths which only work could reveal. As the tree of life gave food to the flesh, and reminded constantly of the mental and spiritual food necessary, so manual training added light to the mental discipline. The laws of the physical, mental, and spiritual world were enunciated; man's threefold nature received attention. This was education, perfect and complete.

The magnetic power about the tree of life held man, filling his senses with a thrill of delight. Adam and Eve lived by that power, and the human mind was an open channel for the flow of God's thought. Rapidly the character of the Edenic pair was being formed, but strength could not come from mere automatic action. Freedom to choose God's company and spirit was given; and while He wooed them with His tenderest love, He had placed in the midst of the garden a tree of another sort.

To the man He said, "Of the tree of the knowledge of good and evil, thou shalt not eat of it; for in the day that thou eatest thereof thou shalt surely die."[11] What was the meaning of this command? As the angel teachers heard the question from man's lips, a cloud seemed to dim the brightness of their glory. Did not Adam feel a strange sensation, as if the fullness of divine thought was suddenly checked in its course through his brain? He was preparing himself to accept teachings of a different character. Then was told the story of the one sorrow heaven had known—of the fall of Lucifer, and the darkness it brought to him; that while he lived, the decree of God was that he could no longer remain within the walls of Paradise. In low tones it was told how some could not see the justice of this; that Lucifer had been given the earth as his present home; that he would use his arts to capture them; but that light and power had been placed about the tree of life, and remaining true to the teaching given within the circle of its rays, no evil could overtake them. "Faith, have faith in God's word," said the angel as he winged his flight toward heaven. The word "death" sounded unnatural to human ears, and as they sat together talking of the angel's words, a longing to understand filled their hearts.

Fear?—they knew no such word. Was not their Maker *love*? Eve, wandering from her husband's side, found, before she knew it, that she was nearing the tree of the knowledge of good and evil. She stood gazing from a distance, when from the rich verdure came a voice of sweetest music:—

"Beautiful woman, made in God's own image, what can mar thy perfect beauty? What can stop that life now coursing through thy veins? 'Hath God said, Ye shall not eat of every tree of the garden?...Ye shall not surely die: for God doth know that in the day ye eat thereof, then your eyes shall be opened, and ye shall be as gods knowing good and evil.' " Speaking, he plucked and ate. Was this the deceiver? Had she not been promised a knowledge of all things? Was she not to be with God? Perhaps this was some new revelation of his goodness. She felt no danger. He ate, why should not she?

Her curiosity was aroused, and she was flattered by the words of the serpent. Instead of fleeing, she argued with him, and attempted to decide in her own mind between right and wrong. But God had told her what was right. That moment of indecision, of doubting, was the devil's opportunity.

Unable to reach the soul of man by direct means, Satan approached it through those outer channels, the senses. He had everything to win, and proceeded cautiously. If man's *mind* could be gained, his great work would be accomplished. To do this, he used a process of reasoning—a method the reverse of that used by the Father in his instruction at the tree of life. The mind of Eve was strong, and quickly drew conclusions; hence, when her new teacher said, "If *ye* eat, 'ye shall be as gods,' " in the mind of Eve arose the thought, God has immortality. "Therefore," said Satan, "if ye eat, 'ye shall not surely die.' " The conclusion was logically drawn, and the world, from the days of Eve to the present time, has based its religious belief on that syllogism, the major premise of which, as did Eve, they fail to recognize as false. Why? Because they use the mind to decide the truth instead of taking a direct statement from the Author of wisdom. From this one false premise comes the doctrine of the natural immortality of man, with its endless variations, some modern names of which are theosophy, Spiritualism, reincarnation, and evolution. The sons and daughters of Eve condemn her for the mistake made six thousand years ago, while they themselves repeat it without question. It is preached from the pulpit, it is taught in the schoolroom, and its spirit pervades the thought of every book written whose author is not in perfect harmony with God and truth. Now began the study of "dialectics," so destructive to the Christian's faith.

Having accepted the logic of the serpent, and having transferred her faith from the word of God to the tree of knowledge at Satan's suggestion, the woman could easily be led to test the truth of all his statements by her senses. A theory had been advanced; the experimental process now began. That is the way men now gain their knowledge, but their wisdom comes otherwise. She looked upon the forbidden fruit, but no physical change was perceptible as the result of the misuse of this sense. This led her to feel more sure that the argument used had been correct. Her ears were attentive to the words of the serpent, but she perceived no change as a result of the perverted use of the sense of hearing. This, to the changing mind of the woman, was still more conclusive proof that the words of Christ and angels did not mean what she had at first thought they meant. The senses of touch, smell, and taste were in turn used, and each corroborated the conclusion drawn by the devil. The woman was deceived, and through the deception her mind was changed. This same change of mind may be wrought either by deception or as a result of false reasoning.

Eve approached Adam with the fruit in her hand. Instead of answering in the oft-repeated words of Christ, "In the day that thou eatest thereof thou shalt surely die," he took up the logic of the serpent. Having eaten, his mind was also changed. He who from creation had thought the thoughts of God, was yielding to the mind of the enemy. The exactness with which he had once understood the mind of God was exemplified when he named the animals; for the thought of God which formed the animal passed through the mind of Adam, and "whatsoever Adam called every living creature, that was the name thereof."

The completeness of the change which took place is seen in the argument used when God walked in the garden in the cool of the evening. Said Adam, "The woman gave me to eat. Thou gavest me the woman. Therefore, Thou art to blame." This was another decidedly logical conclusion, from the standpoint of the wisdom of the serpent, and it was repeated by Eve, who laid the blame first on the serpent, and finally on God himself. Self-justification, self-exaltation, self-worship—here was the human origin of the papacy, that power which "opposeth and exalteth itself above all that is called God."

The spiritual death which followed the perversion of the senses was attended, in time, by physical death. Indeed, the fruit had scarcely been eaten when the attention of the man and his wife was turned toward externals. The soul, which had enveloped the physical man as a shroud of light, withdrew, and the physical man appeared. A sense of their nakedness now appalled them. Something was lacking; and with all the glory they had known, with all the truths which had been revealed, there was nothing to take the place of the departed spiritual nature. "Dying, thou shalt die," was the decree; and had not the Saviour at this moment made known to Adam the plan of the cross, eternal death would have been inevitable.

God, through His instruction, had taught that the result of faith would be immortal life. Satan taught, and attempted to prove his logic by a direct appeal to the senses, that there was immortal life in the wisdom that comes as the result of human reason. The method employed by Satan is that which men today call the natural method, but in the mind of God the wisdom of the world is foolishness. The method which to the godly mind, to the spiritual nature, seems natural, is foolishness to the world.

There are but two systems of education—the one based on what God calls wisdom, the gift of which is eternal life; the other based on what the world regards as wisdom, but which God says is foolishness. This last exalts reason above faith, and the result is spiritual death. That the fall of man was the result of choosing the false system of education cannot be controverted. Redemption comes through the adoption of the true system of education.

Re-creation is a change of mind—an exchange of the natural for the spiritual. "Be not conformed to this world, but be ye transformed by the renewing of your mind." In order to render such a change possible, Christ must bruise the head of the serpent; that is, the philosophy of the devil must be disproved by the Son of God. Christ did this, but in so doing, his heel, representing his physical nature, was bruised. The result of the acceptance of the satanic philosophy has been physical suffering; and the more completely man yields to the system built upon that philosophy, the more complete is the subjection of the race to physical infirmities.

After the fall, man turned to coarser articles of diet, and his nature gradually became more gross. The spiritual nature, at first the prominent part of his being, was dwarfed and overruled until it was but the "small voice" within. With the development of the physical and the intellectual to the neglect of the spiritual, have come the evils of modern society—the love of display, the perversion of taste, the deformity of the body, and those attendant sins which destroyed Sodom, and now threaten our cities. Man became careless in his work also, and the earth failed to yield her fullness. As a result, thorns and thistles sprang up.

It is not surprising, after following the decline of the race, to find that the system of education introduced by Christ begins with the instruction given in the garden of Eden, and that it is based on the simple law of faith. We better appreciate the gift of Christ when we dwell upon the thought that while suffering physically, while taking our infirmities into his own body, He yet preserved a sound mind and a will wholly subject to the Father's, that by so doing the philosophy of the archdeceiver might be overthrown by the divine philosophy.

Again, it is but natural to suppose that when called upon to decide between the two systems of education, the human and the divine, and Christian education is chosen, that man will also have to reform his manner of eating and living. The original diet of man is again made known, and for his home he is urged to choose a garden spot, away from crowded cities, where God can speak to his spiritual nature through His works. God does use the senses of man; but *knowledge* thus gained becomes *wisdom* only when enlightened by the Spirit, the gateway to whose fountain is opened by the key of faith.

Beneath the tree of life originated the highest method of education—the plan the world needs today. Beneath the branches of the tree of the knowledge of good and evil arose the conflicting system, having ever one object in view—the overthrow of the eternal principles of truth. Under one guise, then under another, it has borne sway upon the earth. Whether as Babylonish learning, Greek philosophy, Egyptian wisdom, the high glitter of papal pomp, or the more modest but no less subtle workings of modern science, the results always have been, and always will be, a savor of death unto death.

As was the unassuming life of the Saviour of man when walking the earth unrecognized by the lordly Pharisees and wise men of his day, so has been the progress of truth. It has kept steadily on the onward march, regardless of oppression. Men's minds, clouded by self-worship, fail to recognize the voice from heaven. It is passed by as the low mutterings of thunder at the gate Beautiful when the Father spoke to his Son, and the halo of heavenly light encircling eternal truth is explained by natural causes. Man's reason is opposed to simple faith, but those who will finally reach the state of complete harmony with God will have begun where Adam failed. Wisdom will be gained by faith. Self will have been lost in the adoration of the great Mind of the universe, and he who was created in the image of God, who was pronounced by the Master Mind as "*very good,*" will, after the struggle with sin, be restored to the harmony of the universe by the simple act of faith.

"If thou canst believe, all things are possible."

Chapter IV
The History of Fifteen Centuries

As a stone, hurled from some mountain peak, crashes its way toward the valley beneath, gaining velocity with each foot of descent, until, wrapped within it, lies a power of destruction unmeasured, so man, turning from the gate of Paradise, began a downward career which in intensity and rapidity can be measured only by the height from which he started.

Giant minds held mighty powers in abeyance. Before the strong will of men of the first ten centuries few forces could stand. As the plane to which it was possible for him to attain was perfection, so the level to which he descended was confusion itself. Men's lives, instead of being narrowed by the brief span of threescore years and ten, were measured by centuries; and intellects, mighty by birth, had time as well as power to expand. The man of seventy was then but a lad, with life and all its possibilities spread out before him. Adam lived to see his children to the eighth generation; and when we think that from his own lips Enoch learned the story of the fall, of the glories of the Eden home; when we bear in mind that Enoch probably saw this same ancestor laid in the earth, there to molder to dust, we better understand the relation he desired to sustain to his God. After a life of three hundred years, in which, the Sacred Record says, he "walked with God," earth's attraction grew so slight that he himself was taken into heaven. This was less than sixty years after the death of Adam. Passing beyond the gate of Eden, two classes of minds developed. Clear and distinct as light from darkness was the difference between the two. Cain, by exalting his own reasoning powers, accepted the logic of Satan. Admitting the physical plane to be the proper basis for living, he lost all appreciation of spiritual things, and depended wholly upon feeling. True, for a time he adhered to the form of worship, coming week by week to the gate of Eden to offer sacrifice; but his eye of faith was blind. When he saw his brother's sacrifice accepted, a feeling of hatred sprang up in his breast, and, raising his hand, he took that brother's life. Men are startled at the rapidity of the descent from Edenic purity to a condition where murder was easy, but it was the natural result of the educational system chosen by Cain. Reason exalted above faith makes man like the engine without the governor.

Murder, however, was but one result of the decision made by Cain. He fled from the presence of God, and, with his descendants built the cities of the East. Physical needs predominated, so that the whole attention of this people was turned to the gratification of fleshly desires. Pride increased, love of wealth was a ruling passion; the artificial took, more and more, the place once occupied by the natural. In the place of God-worship was self-worship, or paganism. This was the religious aspect, and here are to be found the first worshipers of the sun, the human progenitors of the modern papacy.

As there was a change in religion, so there was a change in government. There could no longer be a theocracy, the father of the family being the high priest unto God; for God had been lost sight of, and his place was filled by man himself. Hence, these descendants of Cain flocked together into cities, where the strong bore rule over the weak, and thus developed an absolute monarchy, which is perpetuated today in the kingdoms of eastern Asia.

The education which upheld paganism in religion and monarchy in government was the same as that which in later days controlled Greece, and is known by us today as Platonism. It is but another name for an education which exalts the mind of man above God, and places human philosophy ahead of divine philosophy.

The philosophy which was thus exalted—this science falsely so-called—deified nature, and would today be known as evolution. You think the name a modern one. It may be, but the philosophy antedates the flood, and the schools of those men before the flood taught for truth the traditions of men as truly as they are taught today.

We think, perhaps, that there were no schools then, but that is a mistake. "The training of the youth in those days was after the same order as children are being educated and trained in this age—to love excitement, to glorify themselves, to follow the imaginations of their own evil hearts." Their keen minds laid hold of the sciences; they delved into the mysteries of nature.

They made wonderful progress in inventions and all material pursuits. But the imaginations of their hearts were only evil continually.

Children educated in the cities had their evil tendencies exaggerated. The philosophical teaching of the age blotted out all faith; and when Noah, a teacher of righteousness, raised his voice against the popular education, and proclaimed his message of faith, even the little children scoffed at him.

So polluted were the cities that Enoch chose to spend much time in retired places, where he could commune with God, and where he would be in touch with nature. At times he entered the cities, proclaiming to the inhabitants the truth given to him by God. Some listened, and occasionally small companies sought him in his places of retirement, to listen to his words of warning. But the influence of early training, the pressure brought to bear by society, and the philosophy of the schools, exerted a power too strong to resist, and they turned from the pleadings of conscience to the old life.

As Noah told of the coming flood, and as he and his sons continued to build the ark, men and children derided. "Water from heaven! Ah, Noah, you may talk of your spiritual insight, but who ever heard of water coming out of the sky? The thing is an impossibility; it is contrary to all reason, to all scientific truth, and to all earth's experience. You may think such things were revealed to you; but since the days of our father Adam, no such thing ever happened." Such statements seemed true. Generation after generation had looked into a sky undarkened by storm-clouds. Night after night dew watered the growing plants. Why should they believe otherwise?

They could see no *reason* for it. To those antediluvians, the possibility of a flood seemed as absurd as does its recital as a matter of history to the modern higher critic. It was out of harmony with men's senses, hence an impossibility.

The student in the nineteenth century finds in the earth's crust great beds of coal, or the remains of monsters which once lived upon the face of the earth, and he accounts for these by saying that "*time is long.*" In the words of Dana, "If time from the commencement of the Silurian age included *forty-eight millions* of years, which *some geologists would pronounce much too low* an estimate, the Paleozoic part, according to the above ratio, would comprise thirty-six million, the Mesozoic nine millions, and the Cenozoic three millions." Modern text-books are filled with these and related ideas of evolution, which account for the effects of the flood by gradual changes consuming millions of years.

The Word of God is again laid aside, and man by his own power of reasoning draws conclusions contrary to the testimony of the Inspired Record. The theory of evolution is thus substantiated in the human mind; and as the antediluvians were, by their scientific research and wisdom, falsely so-called, unfitted to receive the message of the flood, so people today, by pursuing a similar course, are unfitting themselves for the message of Christ's appearance in the clouds of heaven. When will man learn that there are things which eye hath not seen, nor ear heard, and yet which exist as really as do those *few things*—few compared with the *many* in the regions beyond—which fall within our range of vision?

Before the flood, no peal of thunder had ever resounded among the hills, no lightning had ever played through the heavens. You who today have read the works of earth's greatest authors, who have delved into the secrets of science, have you discovered the soul of man? Have you yet found the golden cord of faith? Should the Almighty question you as He did His servant Job, how would you pass the examination? To you would befall the fate of the generation of Noah. Four men built the ark. Such a thing had never been seen before. "How unshapely" say they. "How absurd to think of water standing over the earth *until that will float!*" But in the ears of the faithful four whispered the still, small voice of God, and the work went steadily on.

The controversy was an educational problem. Christian education was almost wiped from the earth. Worldly wisdom seemed about to triumph. In point of numbers its adherents vastly exceeded those in the schools of the Christians. Was this seeming triumph of evil over good a sign that evil was stronger than truth? By no means. Only in the matter of scheming and deceiving does the devil have the advantage; for God can work only in a straightforward manner.

The tree of life was still upon the earth, an emblem of the wisdom of God. Man, however, had turned his back upon it. Eating the fruit of the tree of knowledge of good and evil brought death, and this the inhabitants of the earth were about to realize, although their worldly wisdom taught them the contrary.

The tree of life was taken to heaven before the flood,[12] thus symbolizing the departure of true wisdom from the earth. The flood came. Deep rumblings of thunder shook the very earth. Man and beast fled terrified from the flashes of lightning. The heavens opened; the rain fell—at first in great drops. The earth reeled and cracked open; the fountains of the great deep were broken up; water came from above, water from beneath. A cry went up to heaven, as parents clasped their children in the agony of death; but the Spirit of the Life-giver was withdrawn. Does this seem cruel? God had pleaded with each generation, with each individual, saying, "Why will ye, why will ye?" But only a deaf ear was turned to Him. Man, satisfied with schooling his senses, with depending upon his own reasoning powers, closed, one by one, every avenue through which the Spirit of God could work; and nature, responding to the loss, was broken to her very heart, and wept floods of tears.

One family, and only one, bound heaven and earth together. Upon the bosom of the waters rocked the ark in safety. God's Spirit rested there, and in the midst of greater turmoil than angels had ever witnessed, a peace which passeth all under-standing filled the minds and hearts of that faithful company.

The waters subsided; the earth lay a desolate mass. Mountains stood bleak and barren where once stretched plains of living green. Trees, magnificent in their towering strength, lay dying as the waters left the earth. Great mass-es of rock covered places hitherto inhabited. This family came forth as strangers in a strange land.

The plan of education must start anew. Each successive step away from God rendered more difficult man's access to his throne; it had lengthened, as it were, the ladder one more round. There was at first this *one* lesson to be tak-en by faith—that God was true in saying, "In the day that thou eatest thereof thou shalt surely die." It was a lesson of faith versus reason. Next came *two* lessons of faith: first, faith opposed by reason; and, second, the plan of redemp-tion through Christ. Then came the *third* lesson—the flood. Would that man could have grasped the first, or, missing that, he had taken the second, or even losing hold of that, he could have taken the third by faith, and prevented the flood.

From beginning to end it was a matter of education. Christians today exalt the material to the neglect of the spiri-tual, as surely as did men before the flood. Shall we not look for similar results, since similar principles are at work?

The education of the popular schools advocated nature study; but, leaving God out, they deified nature, and ac-counted for the existence of all things by the same theories which are today termed evolution. This is man's theory of creation with faith dropped out of the calculation.

"This they willingly are ignorant of, that by the word of God the heavens were of old, and the earth standing out of the water and in the water: whereby the world that then was, being overflowed with water, perished: but the heav-ens and the earth, which are now, by the same word are kept in store, reserved unto fire against the day of judgment."[13]

"As it was in the days of Noah, so shall it be also in the days of the Son of man."[14]

Chapter V
The School of Abraham

THE ease with which men fall into evil habits is illustrated in the history of the world after the flood. Upon leaving the ark, four families who had known God, had committed to them the peopling of the earth. But evil tendencies, the result of years of acquaintance with the iniquity of the antediluvian world, gained the ascendancy, and the sons of Noah, failing to carry out the principles of true education in their homes, saw their children drifting away from God.

True, the bow of promise appeared often in the heavens as a reminder of the awful results of sin, and telling them also of the God-Father who sought their hearts' service. But again, the logic of the evil one was accepted, and men said, "We shall not surely die." As a sign of their confidence in their own strength they built the tower of Babel. They had been scattered in the hill country, where nature and natural scenery tended to elevate their thoughts. They followed the valley, and built cities in the low plains.

Not more than a single century had elapsed since the flood had destroyed all things. The change was a rapid one. The successive steps in degeneration are readily traced. They chose an education of the senses rather than one of faith; they left the country and congregated in cities; a monarchy arose.

Schools sprang up which perpetuated these ideas; paganism took the place of the worship of God. The tower was a monument to the sun; idols filled the niches in the structure. Men offered their children as sacrifices.

The slaying of infants and children is but carrying out in the extreme what is always done mentally and spiritually when children are taught false philosophy. That man might not bring upon himself immediate destruction, the language was confused, and education in false philosophy thus rendered more difficult.

It was from this influence, as found in the city of Ur of the Chaldees, that Abraham was called. Although the family of Terah knew the true God, and His worship was maintained in the home, it was impossible for him to counteract the influence of the city with its idolatrous practices; so God called Abraham into the country.

He was obliged to go forth by faith. The removal meant the severing of every earthly tie. Wealth and ease were exchanged for a wandering life. How he could make a living Abraham did not know. How he could educate his children he did not understand. But, he went forth. Terah, his father, and Lot, his nephew, went with him. They halted at Haran, a smaller city, and remained there until the father's death. Then came the command to go forward. Out into a new country he went, a pilgrim and a stranger.

"By faith Abraham, when he was called to go out into a place which he should after receive for an inheritance, obeyed; and he went out, not knowing whither he went. By faith he sojourned in the land of promise, as in a strange country, dwelling in tabernacles with Isaac and Jacob, the heirs with him of the same promise; for he looked for a city which hath foundations, whose builder and maker is God." "He staggered not at the promise of God through unbelief; but was strong in faith."[15]

It was when the patriarch had journeyed into this strange land, and knew not whither he was going, that his work as a teacher began. The commission of Christ to the apostles, "Go ye therefore, and *teach* all nations," was not more emphatic than the command to Abraham. God called him to teach, and he was to be a teacher of nations. To the disciples it was said, "All power is given unto Me;...go ye therefore, and teach all nations." A power was to attend their teaching. Power is synonymous with life; there is no power without life, and a teacher has power in proportion as he *lives* what he wishes to teach.

Abraham was to be a teacher of nations; hence he must have power. Power could come only as the result of a life of faith, and so his whole life was one continual lesson of faith. Each experience made him a more powerful teacher. His faith grew by trial, and only as he mounted round by round the ladder which spanned the gulf twixt heaven and earth, and which had seemed to lengthen with each succeeding generation. A period of not less than twenty-five years—years filled with doubt, fear, anxiety—was necessary to bring him to the place where the name *Abraham*—the father of nations—could be rightly claimed by him. Another quarter of a century rolled over his head, years in which he watched the growth of the child of promise; then the voice of God called him to raise his hand to take the life of that same son. He who had said that in Isaac should all nations of the earth be blessed, now demanded the sacrifice of that life at the father's hand. But He, the Life-giver in the event of the child's birth, was now believed to be the Life-giver should death rob him of his child, and the father faltered not.

These fifty years, with God and angels as teachers, reveal to us, as no other period does, the results of true education, and merit careful attention. If the workings of the Spirit ever wrought changes in the human heart, those changes came to Abraham. It is not strange that when God called the first time the voice seemed far away, and but partially awoke the slumbering soul. As if in a dream, he, his father, his nephew, and his wife, broke away from earthly ties and from the beautiful Chaldean plains, where luxury and learning were daily things of life, and journeyed toward the hill country.

It has been stated before that God teaches by the enunciation of principles, or universal laws, and the spirit which comes by faith enlightens the senses that they may grasp the illustrations of these laws in the physical world.

That is heaven's method of teaching the angelic throng, and it was the method applied before the fall. With Abraham the case was at the beginning far from ideal. Here was a pupil lacking faith. How should he be taught the wisdom of the Eternal? God leads in a mysterious way. As Christ lived His visible life, because the eye of faith was blind in Israel, so, in the time of Abraham, God taught inductively, as He now says the heathen are to be taught. To him who had no faith, God came visibly at first, and, leading step by step, developed a faith which before his death enabled Abraham to grasp eternal principles of truth if God but spoke.

In Ur, God said, "I will make of thee a great nation, and I will bless thee, and will make thy name great." Years passed, age crept on, and still there was no heir. Could he have mistaken the voice which bade him turn his face toward Canaan, and promised to him and his descendants all the land from the "great river, the river Euphrates...unto the great sea toward the going down of the sun"? "And Abraham said, Lord God, what wilt Thou give me, seeing I go childless? Shall it be that my steward, Eliezer, shall become my heir? Shall he be the child of promise? Behold, to me Thou hast given no seed and, lo, one born in my house is mine heir."[16]

This was man's way of working out a promise made by the Maker of the universe. Have *we* passed beyond this elementary lesson of faith? Can *we* grasp God's promise of faith, and, with no fear or thought, leave results with Him who knows?

No, Abraham; think not that heaven is limited by the line which bounds thy horizon. "This shall not be thine heir; but he that shall come forth out of thine own bowels shall be thine heir." And, standing under the starry canopy of heaven, Abraham's soul grasped the power of the Creator. He himself to be a father! His face lighted with a holy joy as he related to Sarai his experience with God.

But Sarai bare him no children; and that she might help heaven fulfill its promise, she forsook the divine law of marriage, and gave to Abraham her handmaid, Hagar, to be his wife. Would that man could grasp at least the beginnings of the possibilities of God! Untold suffering was the out-growth of that one step of unbelief. Not one, not two people, but generations then unborn, had their destinies marred by this lack of faith. Hagar, sitting over against her dying child, and weeping because of the bitterness of her fate, is a constant portrayal of an attempt to live by sight.[17] Again, the approach of the angel and the rescue of the child records in burning characters the longing of Him who pities our blindness, and awards us far above what we can ask or think.

Ninety-nine years passed over the patriarch's head, and still the voice of heaven's messenger was greeted with a laugh when the promise was repeated. Sarah turned within the tent door when the angel guest, whom they had fed, repeated to Abraham the promise concerning his wife. But she bare to Abraham a son whom God named Isaac, in whom the nations of the earth were blessed. Joy untold filled the heart of the mother and father as they beheld the babe.

This was the joy of sight. Twenty-five years before, the thing was just as true, and Abraham might lawfully have worked upon the basis of its truth; but the stubborn human heart requires many lessons. Twenty-five years after this, the strength of Abraham's faith was tested at the altar of sacrifice. Leaving home early one morning, he carried fire, laid wood upon the young man's shoulders, and journeyed toward Mount Moriah. "Behold the fire and the wood; but where is the lamb for a burnt offering?" asked the son. "God will provide himself a lamb," answered the man who had at last learned to believe God. It is but the simple story of an ancient patriarch; but the word of God bears record that "Abraham believed God, and it was counted to him for righteousness."

And "if *ye* be Christ's, then are ye Abraham's seed and heirs according to the promise." Herein lies the value of this lesson to us. We are his heirs if we link ourselves to the power of the Infinite by that cord of faith. Only by a life and an education such as his can the kingdom of Christ be set up within. Such lessons made Abraham a successful teacher.

Those who wished to worship the true God gathered about the tents of Abraham, and became pupils in his school. God's word was the basis of all instruction, as it is written, "These are the commandments... which the Lord your God commanded to teach you, that ye might do them in the land whither ye go to possess it."

This Word was the basis for the study of political science, and Abraham's "methods of government" were "carried out in the households over which they [his students] should preside." The equality of all men was a lesson first learned in the home. "Abraham's affection for his children and his household led him... to impart to them a knowledge of the divine statutes, as the most precious legacy he could transmit to them, and through them to the world. All were taught that they were under the rule of the God of heaven. There was to be no oppression on the part of parents, and no disobedience on the part of children." His was not a school where theory alone was taught, but the practical was emphasized. In studying political science, they formed the nucleus of a divine government; in the study of finances, they actually made the money and raised the flocks which brought recognition from surrounding nations. "The unswerving integrity, the benevolence and unselfish courtesy, which had won the admiration of kings, *were displayed in the home.*"

The influence of country life and direct contact with nature, in contrast with the enervating influence of the city with its idolatrous teaching and artificial methods, developed a hardy race, a people of faith whom God could use to lay the foundation for the Israelitish nation. We see, then, that when God founds a nation, he lays that foundation in a school. The nation of which Abraham and his followers formed the beginning, prefigured the earth redeemed, where Christ will reign as King of kings. The education of the school of Abraham symbolized Christian education.

"If ye be Christ's, then are ye Abraham's seed, and heirs according to the promise," not only to the kingdom, but of the education which prepares the inhabitants for that kingdom.

As faith was the method employed in teaching in the days of the patriarch, so in the schools of today faith must be the motive for work, the avenue to the fountain of wisdom. There are today those who cannot harmonize their feelings and their ideas of education with the plan which God has committed to his people. Likewise, in the days of Abraham, there was at least one family which withdrew from the influence of the school.

Lot had felt the effects of the teaching of Abraham, but through the influence of his wife, "a selfish, irreligious woman," he left the altar where they once worshiped together, and moved into the city of Sodom. "The marriage of Lot, and his choice of Sodom for a home, were the first links in a chain of events fraught with evil to the world for many generations." Had he alone suffered, we would not need to follow the history; but the choice of a new home threw his children into the schools of the heathen; pride and love of display were fostered, marriage with Sodomites was a natural consequence, and their final destruction in the burning city was the terrible but inevitable result.

"When Lot entered Sodom, he fully intended to keep himself free from iniquity, and to command his household after him. But he signally failed. The corrupting influences about him had an effect upon his own faith, and his children's connection with the inhabitants of Sodom bound up his interests in a measure with theirs."

The statement is a familiar one, that schools should be established where an education differing from that of the world can be given, because parents are unable to counteract the influence of the schools of the world. The experience of Lot is a forcible reminder of the truth of the statement. And the injunction to "remember Lot's wife," should serve as a warning to Christians against flocking into the cities to give children an education. The words of Spalding are true: "Live not in a great city, for a great city is a mill which grinds all grain into flour. Go there to get money or to preach repentance, but go not there to make thyself a nobler man."

The two systems of education are nowhere more vividly portrayed than in the experiences of Abraham and Lot. Education in the tents of Abraham, under the guidance of the Spirit of Jehovah, brought eternal life. Education in the schools of Sodom brought eternal death. This was not an unnatural thing. You cannot find here any arbitrary work on the part of God. To partake of the fruit of the tree of life, imparts life. But of the tree of knowledge of good and evil it has been said, "In the day that thou eatest thereof thou shalt surely die." The system of education revealed to Abraham, would, if fully carried out, have placed Israel on a plane of existence above the nations of the world. It was a spiritual education, reaching the soul by a direct appeal to faith, and would have placed the people of God as teachers of nations. Not a few only were intended to teach, but the nation as a whole was to teach other nations. The second Israel will occupy a similar position, and they will be brought to that position by means of Christian education.

Chapter VI
Education in Israel

THEREFORE sprang there even of one, and him as good as dead, so many as the stars of the sky in multitude, and as the sand which is by the seashore innumerable." As God dealt with the one man, so He dealt with the nation. As He had led the man from a lowly plane to an exalted position, so He led the nation until they stood a spectacle to the whole world. He chose them not because of their great numbers, but, taking the fewest of men, He wished to show to the world what could be done by the power of love.

This small people, however, were intended to lead the world, and lead it in every sense of the word. That they might lead instead of being led, He made them a peculiar people unto Himself, giving them in the first place the rite of circumcision, which put a barrier forever between the believer in the God of Israel and all the nations of the world. This separation was for a purpose. The fact that they were to be peculiar in the eyes of the other nations was merely a precautionary step, not a thing of importance in itself. God had a mission for the nation; and in order that it might be accomplished, every effort must be bent in that direction. Oneness of purpose is a divine law; and that Israel might lead, Israel must occupy a position in advance of all other peoples.

Men live on various planes. There are those so constituted physically as to be content with the gratification of physical wants and desires. These can readily be led by men who live on a mental plane; for mind has ever been recognized as superior to matter, so that without knowing it, the physically strong yields to his mental superior. Almost unconscious of his power, the man on the mental plane guides and controls those on the physical plane; he cannot help it. It is a natural law; the one leads, the other follows. Two individuals, one living in one of these spheres and the other in the sphere above, will never contend on account of principle; for the man physically organized finds it natural to follow the dictates of the other. This is, and always has been, the condition of society. Nature herself singles out the leaders. They are born, not made, for leadership. They are the few, it is true; the masses always prefer to be led.

But it was not as mere mental leaders that God called Israel. There is above the mental a still higher plane, the ladder to reach which is scaled by very few. As the numbers decrease while passing from the physical to the mental plane, so they decrease yet more in passing from the mental to the *spiritual* plane.

Man reaches this highest plane of existence only by faith. It requires constant self-denial and continual development. In reality it is living as seeing Him who is invisible. The physical man depends almost entirely on knowledge gained through the senses. The mentally developed depends upon reason.

Many combine these two natures, and such individuals are guided by the sense of reason just in proportion as the two natures are developed.

Knowledge as a result of sense perceptions and finite reason capture the majority of mankind. The life of faith, the walking with God, takes in the few.

Do you see why God chose a small people? He chose them, as a nation, to be priests or teachers unto Himself. As individuals, and as a nation, Israel was to stand upon the spiritual plane, attaining and maintaining the position by a life of faith. Standing there, it would be in accordance with the natural law for all on the lower planes to yield obedience. As the mental controls the physical without any friction, so the spiritual controls all others.

Therefore (for this reason) said the Lord, "I have taught you statutes and judgments....Keep therefore and do them; for this is your wisdom and your understanding in the sight of the nations, which shall hear all these statutes, and say, Surely this great nation *is a wise and understanding people.*"[18]

Statutes in themselves cannot command respect for any people, but God gave Israel a manner of life which linked them with Himself. Living on a spiritual plane, all the world looked to them for guidance. As one cannot reach up and help those above him, but must come from above and lift others to himself, so Israel was pointed to a life which made others follow in spite of themselves, while at the same time they were following what they knew to be the truth. This is the exalted position which truth has ever held.

Granting it clear that Israel would lead by virtue of the plane of existence upon which they stood, and that this was attained by a life of faith, it is easily seen why there was marked out for the nation a *system of education* differing as completely from the systems of the other nations of the world as the spiritual life differs from a purely physical or a strictly mental existence. It made it impossible for any mingling of systems to take place without the utter ruin of the spiritual; for as soon as this came down to the level of either of the others, it ceased to be spiritual, and lost its power to lead.

Should Israel attempt to adopt the education of surrounding nations, that moment her education would become papal in character, for it would then be a combination of the divine with the worldly. If a man-made theocracy, a church and state government, is papal in principle, the divine and the worldly combined in educational systems is no less a papal principle. Israel formed such a combination more than once, but with the results recorded in Ps. 106:34-38: "They mingled among the heathen, and learned their works. And they served their idols: which were a snare unto them. Yea, they sacrificed their *sons* and their *daughters* unto devils, and shed innocent blood, even the blood of their sons and of their daughters, whom they sacrificed unto the idols of Canaan."

Truth and error never form a compound, although they may be mingled. The union of the two never produces truth, and the end is death. Truth amalgamated with error, as gold with mercury, lies dormant until released. Israel could not positively forsake her God-given forms of education without relinquishing her place as leader of nations. Destined to be the head and not the tail, she immediately reversed her position when she adopted a mixed system.

The education which was outlined for the children of Israel was soul-culture, pure and simple. Its object was to develop the soul which is God in man; and Divinity so planned that every true Jew should be a God-man.

Education was to develop the spark of divinity bestowed at birth, and it was the privilege of every Jew to have, as did that *One* Jew, Christ, the Spirit without measure.

Let us see, then, what the plan was which would take the newborn babe, and follow him through life, making him one unit in a nation of spiritual beings. God recognized prenatal influence, and so gave directions and laws concerning the life of the parents. This is illustrated in the story of Hannah, and the wife of Manoah, in Elizabeth, and in Mary the mother of Jesus.

In the early history of the nation, "Education," says Painter, "was restricted to the family, in which the father was the principal teacher. There were no popular schools nor professional teachers. Yet the instruction of the Jew... embraced a vast number of particulars."[19] Hinsdale says: "Jewish education began with the mother. What the true Jewish mother, considered as a teacher, was, we know from both the Testaments and from many other sources. The very household duties that she performed molded her children in accordance with the national discipline. 'The Sabbath meal, the kindling of the Sabbath lamp, and the setting apart of a portion of the dough from the bread for the household—these are but instances with which every *Taph,* as he clung to his mother's skirts, must have been familiar.' The bit of parchment fastened to the doorpost, on which the name of the Most High was written...would be among the first things to arrest his attention.

"It was in the school of the mother's knee that the stories of patriarchs and prophets, of statesmen and warriors, of poets and sages, of kings and judges, wise men and patriots, and of the great Law-giver Himself—the whole forming the very best body of material for the purposes of child-nurture found in any language—were told and retold until they became parts of the mind itself." He then mentions the case of Timothy, and adds: "As teachers of their children, the women of every country may learn lessons from the matrons of Israel."[20] This was evidently the original plan, and had the families proved faithful to the trust, the greater part, if not all, of the education would have been in the *family school*. Always, however, as long as Israel was a nation, the child (and the term covered the first twelve or fifteen years) was under the instruction of the parents.

From the home school we follow the Jewish child to the synagogue or church school. Moses was instructed by the Lord to make every priest a teacher, so the nation had a whole tribe of teachers. As every town had its synagogue, so "a town in which there is no school must perish." Quoting again from Hinsdale: "The children were gathered for instruction in the synagogues and schoolhouses, where the teacher, generally the Chazzan, or officer of the synagogue, 'imparted to them the precious knowledge of the law, with constant adaptation to their capacity, with unwearied patience, intense earnestness, strictness tempered by kindness, but, above all, with the highest object of their training ever in view. *To keep children from all contact with vice; to train them to gentleness, even when bitterest wrong had been received;* to show sin in its repulsiveness, rather than to terrify by its consequences; *to train to strict truthfulness;* to avoid all that might lead to disagreeable or indelicate thoughts; and to do all this without showing partiality, without either undue severity or laxity of discipline, with judicious increase of study and work, with careful attention to thoroughness in acquiring knowledge—all this and more constituted the ideal set before the teacher, and made his office of such high esteem in Israel.' "[21] These teachers took the youth at the most critical period of their development. And how thoroughly they understood the needs of the developing minds!

In the days of Samuel, we read, for the first time, of the schools of the prophets, where young men were gathered together for the study of the law, of music, poetry, and history, and of the various trades. The name *School of the Prophets* would indicate the spirituality of their work, and reference to the time of Elijah and Elisha and the experience of Saul would prove the truth of the inference.

Concerning the subjects taught we are not left in ignorance, if we study the history of the people. Thus, quoting again from Painter: "The Hebrew parent was not only to impart oral instruction to his children, but to teach them also *reading and writing.* As he was to inscribe the words of the Lord upon his doorposts and gates, he must himself have learned to write; and, as he wrote them for his children, they must have been taught to read. Hence, it appears that the ability to read and write was general among the ancient Jews; and, in this particular, they surpassed every other nation of antiquity."[22] Hinsdale says: "From the teaching of the alphabet, or writing in the primary school, to the farthest limit of instruction in the academies of the rabbis, all was marked by extreme care, wisdom, accuracy, and moral and religious purpose as the ultimate object."[23]

"Up to ten years of age the Bible was the sole textbook; from ten to fifteen the *Mischna*, or traditional law, was used; and after that the pupil was admitted to the discussions of the rabbinical schools. So extensive a course of study, however, was taken only by those who showed decided aptitude for learning. Bible study began with the book of Leviticus; then came other parts of the Pentateuch; next the prophets, and finally the Hagiography."[24]

In working for this chosen people, God cured physical infirmities with the same ease that he healed a sin-sick soul; and with the laws for spiritual growth were given directions for the preservation of health. Every priest was likewise a physician, and the laws concerning the use of simple, healthful foods, proper breathing, ventilation, the use of disinfectants, the bath, etc., were familiar to all who read the statutes of Jehovah.

Painter says, concerning other subjects taught: "Among the potent educational agencies of the Jews, that of the annual national festivals merits consideration....Commemorating important national events, they kept the people acquainted with their past *history*....These frequent reunions not only contributed to national and religious unity, but they exerted a strong educating influence upon the people."[25]

"The Levites, more than other Hebrews, were to study the book of the *law*; to preserve and disseminate it in exact copies; to perform the duties of *judges and genealogists*, and consequently to be theologians, jurists, and historians. As the priests and Levites were to test the accuracy of weights and measures,...it was necessary that they should understand something of *mathematics*; and as they were to determine and announce the movable feasts, new moons, years, and intercalary years, they had occasion for the study of *astronomy*," says Jahn.

Since the schools of the prophets flourished in the days of Saul and David, it would not be surprising if David gained some of his musical skill there as well as on the hillside tending sheep, for *poetry and music* formed part of the course of instruction in these schools. One author pays high tribute to these subjects by saying: "Greek poetry is beautiful; Hebrew poetry is sublime."

When children were fortified by such an education from infancy to manhood, it is little wonder that the influence which the nation "has exerted upon the world is incalculable. It has supplied the basis of all true theology; it has given a system of faultless morality; and, in Christianity, it has provided the most perfect form of religion. The civilization of *Europe* and *America* can be directly traced to the Jews."[26]

What might have been the result had the nation lived up to its privileges in educational lines is not difficult to determine. Earth's history would have been shortened by at least two thousand years; for the nation would never have gone into bondage, and Christ would never have been betrayed. As these principles of Christian education are again taking hold of people, with what interest must the progress of the work be watched by the inhabitants of other worlds, who have seen past failures through lack of faith! That Hebrew education tended mainly to a development of the inner man instead of giving merely a conglomeration of facts, is well expressed by Wines. He says: "The Hebrew law required an early, constant, vigorous, and efficient training of the disposition, judgment, manners, and habits, both of thought and feeling. The sentiments held to be proper to man in society were imbibed with the milk of infancy. The manners considered becoming in adults were sedulously imparted in childhood."

The education, however, was not only moral and intellectual, but physical as well; for every Jewish boy was taught some trade which rendered him self-supporting. Nor did wealth or position remove the need of this. Paul, who sat at the feet of Gamaliel while studying the law, was able to gain a livelihood as a tentmaker when preaching the gospel.

There was, however, in it all this one thought: all instruction was intended to develop the spiritual nature. It was considered the highest honor to become a priest (every Jew might have been both priest and teacher), and in this office man stood next to God. This was wholly a spiritual position, and prefigured the work of the Messiah. True, Israel as a nation never reached the standard set for her, never mounted, as it were, that ladder reaching from earth to heaven; and it was left for the One Man, the Master of

Israel, to bind together the two realms of the physical and the spiritual. But from time to time men arose in the Jewish nation who grasped in a far broader sense than the majority, the meaning of true education as delivered to the Jews, and who, by submitting to the educating influence of the Spirit of God, were enabled to become leaders of the people and representatives of God on earth. Such were Moses, Daniel, Job, and Ezekiel, and, to a certain extent, all the prophets of Israel. In each of these the soul rose above the physical man, until it met its parent force in the heart of God. This made it possible for Moses to talk face to face with the Father, and for Ezekiel to follow the angel of revelation to the border land of God's home.

These men were but enjoying what *every man in Israel* might have experienced had the nation remained upon the plane to which they were called, receiving their education by faith. One is tempted to ask why they fell. The answer is the same as to that other question, Why do not we arise? They ceased to look upward; faith failed, and reason took its place, and instead of leading they sought to be like the nations about them. There lay Egypt, with its mighty men, and the carnal heart longed for some of the Egyptian display. To understand it, we must again consider the difference in life and education. Life on the spiritual plane means whole self-forgetfulness; but when carnal desires are heeded, a fall is inevitable.

Egyptian education was largely on the physical basis. It is true that mental heights were reached, but only by the few, and those few, bound by earth's fetters, were unable to break entirely away. The masses, not only in education but in religion, were physical, and *basely physical*. The sacred bull was a personification of deity. Why? Because God, to an Egyptian, was an embodiment of lust. All their gods, all their rites and ceremonies, every temple wall and religious service, breathed the dreadful odor of licentiousness. Historians state that the priestly class knew better. And so they did; but their grasp was not that of truth, else they could never have been the priests and teachers of such a religion or of such a system of education.

These words, put in the mouth of an ancient Egyptian priest, speak truly the spirit of Egyptian education. He says: "I that have seen nigh fourscore years of misery....I that have mastered all the arts, sciences, and religion of ancient Egypt—a land that was wrinkled with age centuries before the era of Moses; I that know both all that the priests of Kem ever taught the people, and also the higher and more recondite forms of ignorance in which the priests themselves believed—I verily know nothing! I can scarcely believe in anything *save universal darkness*, for which no day-spring cometh, and universal wretchedness for which there is no cure. O wretched man that I am, who shall deliver me from this death?"

And yet the Jews would leave that education which offered eternal life, for this which the best-educated Egyptian might acknowledge to be darkness and only darkness. It was from this that God delivered Israel; but many to-day, claiming to be Israel in Spirit, seek still the wisdom and philosophy of Egypt for themselves and their children. Israel could not come in touch with this form of life without contamination. Nay, more, she fell from her exalted state, and never reached it again. "Jerusalem was destroyed because the education of her children was neglected."

The ceremonial law given after leaving Sinai, at the beginning of that memorable march of forty years, was necessary because the nation had lost all appreciation of the spiritual in the abstract, and could gain no idea whatever of God as a *Spirit* except through some appeal to the physical senses. This condition was due to the fact that four generations had been subject to Egyptian education.

The plan of types and ceremonies alone appealed to the mind. And even in this inductive method of teaching, the nation seemed slow to learn; for the forty years between the Red Sea and Jordan served to develop scarcely enough faith to carry the people into the promised land. God's law, written on the tablets of the heart by the pen of faith, appealed to but few. Men ate manna from heaven, but knew not that it was the token of a crucified Saviour: they drank of water flowing constantly from the smitten rock, never dreaming that it prefigured the shed blood of the dying Son of God. Once settled in Canaan, the whole system of education was so planned as to teach the child to accept Christ by faith. Some grasped this spiritual truth; but a few had eyes which saw the things hidden from the multitude, because faith was an avenue to the very soul.

Having the privilege of living by faith, and accepting the divine teaching in this its highest form, they preferred the old way, and walked by sight. "Except ye see, ye will not believe;" "O ye of little faith." When we look at what the Israelites might have been, and then at what they were, there is a feeling of intense pain, for the fall is inexpressibly great. By little and little, Jehovah strove to reach the higher nature again, and bring Israel to its heaven-selected place. There was steady progress until the days of Solomon, whose wisdom outshone that of the great men of earth, and Israel as a nation was again on the verge of becoming the leading people of the world politically, intellectually, and morally.

Solomon was raised to a position of eminence among the great men of earth because he learned from God the secret of true education. His wisdom was not a gift to him exclusively, but was offered to all who would comply with the educational requirements. Of Solomon we read that God gave him a hearing ear. His spiritual senses were awakened by faith, and he found himself so in harmony with the God of nature that all the works of the Creator were read by him as an open book. His wisdom seemed great in contrast with that of other Jews merely because others failed to live up to their privileges. God desired the whole nation to stand before other people as Solomon stood before the kings of the earth.

The surprising feature to most students is the fact that the system of education given by God will, when followed, open to man such material benefits. It is not, as it is often accused of being, ideal and theoretical, but lacking the practical. On the contrary, it is of the most practical nature, and opens to its followers all legitimate lines of prosperity, placing its devotees above all contestants. This is seen in the experience of the king just mentioned. As a statesman and lawyer, Solomon was noted; as a scientist, he excelled the scholars of the world; for wealth and splendor, the half has not been told; during his reign Jewish architecture, as exemplified in the temple, assumed such grandeur that it became the model for even the aesthetic Greek. In tilling the soil and raising fruit it was always intended that Israel should excel other nations.[27] Youth were trained to fill positions of trust, and were taught the practical duties of everyday life. Such training was given to girls as well as to boys, fitting them to fill properly their allotted sphere as housewives and mothers in Israel.[28]

From the fall which followed this exaltation, Israel never recovered. The educational system losing its true character, the nation was at last carried into captivity. When the Hebrew race lost the spirituality of their education, they lost everything; for political power, national reputation, all, hung upon one thread. "Jerusalem was destroyed because the education of her children was neglected." This destruction did not come suddenly. There was a decline, then a forward lunge, and another relapse, each time the fall being greater and the reaction weaker. Several times a halt was made, and the national life was prolonged by a return to the prescribed methods of education. Jehoshaphat, for instance, appointed Levites as teachers to the different cities of Israel, and, as a result, "The fear of the Lord fell upon all the kingdoms of the lands that were round about Judah, so that they made no war."[29] Had the reform been carried on which was then begun, the whole national history would have been changed.

Another noticeable fact is that release from bondage was always heralded by two reforms. For instance, before deliverance from Babylon, Daniel was raised up to give the people instruction in health reform and educational reform. These two always accompany each other. The one affects the body, preparing it to become the temple of the Holy Ghost; the other turns the mind toward truth, that the Spirit of God may think through it. A body purified by right living, and a mind trained according to the laws of Christian education, brings an experience such as Daniel had.[30] That he lived on a plane above the majority of men is evident; for "I, Daniel, alone saw the vision: for the men that were with me saw not the vision." What to Daniel was the voice of God those whose ears were not in tune with the Infinite heard as thunder or as an earthquake. It had been the privilege of all to see and hear as Daniel saw and heard, but they chose a coarser life, a slower vibratory existence, where the mental strain was less, and the heart strings were looser. It was easier to keep in tune with Egypt or Babylon than with the God of heaven. And when the Son of Man was born, he found it hard to select even a small company whose lives were in harmony with His own.

Israel's education was a spiritual education. Her King was to set up a spiritual kingdom in the hearts of a people spiritualized by the presence of truth. It was the same system which had been delivered by Christ to Adam; the same by which Abraham was taught; and what was not accomplished in the ages past will be accomplished by Christian education in the days preparatory to His second coming.

Chapter VII
The Educational System of the Pagan World

GOD called Israel to become a nation of teachers, and gave them statutes and judgments which, when made the basis of the educational systems, tended to make of the nation a peculiar people, a nation of priests, a spiritual race, thereby constituting them the leading people of the world. From what did he call them? "The Lord hath taken you, and brought you forth out of the iron furnace, out of Egypt."[31] And again, "Out of Egypt have I called my Son."[32] Egypt stands as a personification of the heathen world, and its very name means darkness. The dark mantle of paganism has ever obstructed the bright shining of the light of truth.

As Israel's power, physical, intellectual, and political, was derived from, and depended upon, her system of education, so it would be but natural to suppose that the opposing power of paganism would possess educational ideas, and be controlled by a system of instruction in harmony with its practices. Or, to state it more logically, we necessarily conclude that the pagan world rested upon a distinct system of education, and that the customs and practices of pagan nations were the result of the educational ideas which they advocated.

The God-given system, as found among the Hebrews, rested upon faith, and developed the spiritual side of man's nature, making it possible in the highest sense for divinity to unite with humanity. The result of this union of the human and the divine—the Immanuel—is the highest creation of the universe. It in itself was a power before which men and demons bowed.

As to paganism and its system of education, what was the religion of the pagan world? and what were the ideas it strove to propagate? First, it placed above God the study and worship of self. Christ is the "true light that lighteth every man that cometh into the world." All men have, then, at some time in life, light enough to lead them to truth, for the gospel "reveals a divine anger from heaven upon all wickedness and iniquity of men who *pervert the true into the false;* because God having revealed it to them; for from the creation of the world His invisible attributes might be discovered from the created facts—that is, His unseen power and Godhead. Consequently, they are inexcusable."[33]

Men, therefore, who of necessity have light may reject that light, and they then become pagan. Paul, in the first chapter of his Roman letter, states a universal law in that when truth is rejected, error takes its place. The quotation is again taken from Fenton's translation, because the wording, by differing slightly from the authorized version, stimulates thought: "Because, knowing God, they did not honor Him as a God, or rejoice, but trifled in their augmentations, and darkened their senseless hearts; *professing to be philosophers,* they played the fool, and transformed the glory of the imperishable God into an image of perishable man, and birds! and beasts! and reptiles! And, therefore, God abandoned them in the lusts of their hearts to filthiness, to dishonor their own bodies to themselves: they having changed the truth of God into falsehood, by honoring and serving the creature contrary to the Creator, who is truly blessed in all ages."[34]

Having turned from the worship of Jehovah to the worship of man, then bird, beast, and reptile, we find associated with worship the grossest forms of licentiousness. This is stated by Paul in the first chapter of Romans. The thought which must be borne in mind is that man turns from God and worships himself. He can conceive of no power higher than his own mind, no form more lofty than his own. His first idol is the human form, male or female. He endows this with human passions, for he knows no heart but his own. By beholding he becomes changed into the same passionate creature; a beast becomes the personification of his deity, and the sacred bull his god. Everything about the worship is gross, and birds, crocodiles, and all sorts of reptiles become objects of worship. This is Egypt. This, in fact, pictures the final worship in any country which turns from Christ and places faith in man.

There are a variety of forms in worship, as there are a variety of complexions in the men of different countries; but it is one and the same plan throughout, resting upon one system of education, producing the same results, whether traced in the proud Babylonish court, the loathsome filth of Egypt, Greece with its intellectual pride and culture, in Roman law, or in the more modern European countries. Paganism is the green-eyed monster, crouching on the southern shore of the Mediterranean, whose body follows the course of the Nile, whose paws reach both east and west, and whose breath has poisoned the atmosphere of all Europe. Into those eyes men have gazed expecting to find wisdom. It was but the glare of the demon, as the tiger's gaze at night.

For Egypt itself, it blotted out all individual rights, placing the masses as a common herd writhing in superstition under the hands of a tyrannical king and a scheming priesthood. It was indeed "an iron furnace," as God had called it, and as Israel had found by sad experience. It was tyranny in government; it was still more bitter tyranny in education and religion. As well might one strive to move the pyramids, or get words from the silent sphinx, as to hope to change the life in Egypt by means of anything presented in Egypt.

Of Egyptian education, Jahn says: The "priests were a separate tribe…and they performed not only the services of religion but the duties of all civil offices to which learning was necessary. They therefore devoted themselves in a peculiar manner to the cultivation of *the sciences*....

"They studied natural philosophy, natural history, medicine, mathematics (particularly astronomy and geometry), history, civil polity, and jurisprudence." Place this course of study by the side of Jewish education, and you notice in the latter the Bible and such subjects as tended to develop spirituality, those things which faith alone could grasp; while the education of the Egyptian had an entirely intellectual basis, and dealt with those subjects which appeal to the senses and to human reason.

When this system as a system is traced in other countries, especially in Greece, this characteristic becomes startling in the extreme; and if reference is made to it often in contrast to the Jewish system, it is because herein lies the pivot upon which the history of nations revolves. It is either faith or reason today, as it has been faith opposed to reason throughout the ages. In place of reason use the word *philosophy*, for that was a favorite expression among the pagans.

The gospel has stood opposed to the philosophy of the world since the beginning; hence we read, "For the reason of the Cross is certainly folly to the reprobate, but to us, the saved, it is a divine power; for it is written, 'I will destroy the philosophy of the philosophers, and upset the cleverness of the clever.' Where is the philosopher? Where is the scholar? Where is the investigator of this age? Has not God made the *philosophy* of this world folly? For when in the *divine philosophy* the world did not perceive God through the philosophy, it pleased God to save the faithful by means of the folly of preaching. As, however, Jews demand a sign, and Greeks seek after philosophy, we now proclaim a crucified Christ, a certain offense to the Jews, and joke to the heathen, but to the called, whether Jews or Greeks—Christ a divine power and a divine philosophy. For observe your calling, brothers, that there are not many *fashionable philosophers*, nor many powerful men, nor many of high birth."[35]

It is this divine philosophy which the spiritually minded grasp, and which is the sum and substance of their education. It is this human philosophy, or natural philosophy, which in the sight of God is folly, that Egypt and her followers adopted. Minds delving into human philosophy never find God, nor do they approach the realms of divine philosophy. There is a *divine philosophy*, and it is grasped by faith; and there is a human philosophy, a creation of the human mind, a science formulated from deductions which appeal to natural senses. But the man, wisest in human learning alone, remains still a fool in the eyes of God, for the inner man has not been reached.

Our study of pagan education is not, however, confined to the Nile Valley. Indeed, some of the most interesting phases, some of the strongest features of the system, were developed elsewhere. Egypt was the cradle, but Greece and Rome were fields in which these ideas gained strength. We read: "The ancients looked upon Egypt as a school of wisdom. Greece sent thither illustrious philosophers and lawgivers—Pythagoras and Plato, Lycurgus and Solon—to complete their studies." *"Hence, even the Greeks* in ancient times were *accustomed to borrow their politics and their learning* from the Egyptians."[36]

Of the four men mentioned, we look upon Lycurgus as the founder of the Egypt Spartan government, noted for the physical training it gave and the utter subjection of the individual to the state. Every historian recognized this as due to the *system of education* introduced by Lycurgus, and followed out by his people. The newborn babe was adjudged worthy of life or death by a council of the state, the decision being based on the physical condition of the infant. At the age of seven the child became the property of the state, and so remained until sixty. It was more exclusively a physical or purely secular education than that offered elsewhere on earth.

The prosperity of Athens, where was "wrought out the most perfect form of heathen civilization," dates from the time of Solon, who, as we have already learned, *finished his education in Egypt*. In these two men we see the leaning toward the physical side, made so prominent in pagan education. "The course of study in the school of Pythagoras embraced mathematics, physics, metaphysics, and medicine. Especial prominence was given mathematics, which Pythagoras regarded as the noblest science." Here is revealed the inclination of the pagan education toward the purely intellectual. Of Plato we shall read later. If Egypt offered ground for the germination of the seed of pagan education, Greece brought the plant to its seed- producing state; and Rome, acting as the wind with the thistle down, *scattered pagan education broadcast.* Of Rome we read: "It gathered into its arms the elements of Grecian and Oriental culture, and as its end drew nigh, it scatters them freely over the rest of Europe. Rome has been the bearer of culture to the modern world."[37]

In order to understand the fertility of the seeds of pagan education, it is necessary to regard with care the master mind of that system, and this we find in Plato. Emerson, in his "Representative Men," defines his position and the position of his philosophy in the pagan and in the so-called Christian world, making the teachings of this Greek, schooled in Egypt, crowd out the Word of God itself. He says: "Out of Plato come all things that are still written and debated among men of thought....*The Bible* of the learned for twenty-two hundred years, every brisk young man, who says in succession fine things to each reluctant generation (...Erasmus, Bruno, Locke, Rousseau, Coleridge) is some reader of Plato."

That is saying that for twenty-two hundred years Plato and his educational system, known everywhere as Platonism, have taken the *place of the Bible to the leading minds of the world.* "Plato is philosophy, and philosophy, Plato—at once the glory and the shame of mankind, since neither Saxon nor Roman have availed to add any idea to his categories," continues Emerson. "No wife, no children had he, and the *thinkers of all civilized nations are his posterity,* and *are tinged* with his mind. How many great men nature is incessantly sending up out of night, to be *his men—Platonists!*"

Then he gives a list of illustrious names who have stood for learning in the various ages of the world's history, and continues: "Calvinism is in his [Plato's] *Phaedo*: Christianity is in it." How little this writer knew of the power of the truth as given by Christ! Doubtless he formed his judgment from professedly Christian teachers. But he continues: "Mahometanism draws all its philosophy, in its handbook of morals,…from him [Plato]. Mysticism finds in Plato all its texts. This citizen of a town in Greece is no villager nor patriot. An Englishman reads, and says, 'How English!' a German, 'How Teutonic!' an Italian, 'How Roman and how Greek!' " And to show that the recognition of Plato is not stopped by the Atlantic, our versatile New England writer says: "Plato seems, to a reader in New England, an American genius." Has the reader any suspicion that our American educational institutions may have recognized the universality of this master of philosophy, and adopted into their curricula his system of reasoning? One traces, without the aid of magnifiers, the thread of pagan philosophy throughout the American schools.

"As our Jewish Bible has implanted itself in the table talk and household life of every man and woman in the European and American nations, so the writings of Plato have preoccupied *every school of learning, every lover of thought, every church, every poet*—making it impossible to think, *on certain levels, except through him*. He stands between the truth and every man's mind, and has almost impressed language and the primary forms of thought with his name and seal....Here is the germ of that Europe we know so well, in its long history of arts and arms; here are all its traits, already discernible in the mind of Plato....How Plato came thus to be Europe, and philosophy, and almost literature, is the problem for us to solve."[38]

One ceases to wonder that, surrounded as was the Corinthian church by *this philosophy* and in daily touch with these ideas which have swayed the world, Paul wrote to it against accepting the philosophy of men in place of that divine philosophy which he and other apostles were preaching through the cross of Christ. "When I came to you, brethren," writes the apostle, "I came not proclaiming the testimony of God with *grand reasoning or philosophies*, for I decided to know nothing among you except Jesus Christ, and He was crucified....And my thought and my statement were not clothed in captivating *philosophical reasons*; but, in demonstrated spirit and power, so *that your trust might not be in human philosophy*, but in Divine power."[39] "Beware lest any man spoil you *through philosophy* and vain deceit, after the tradition of men, after the elements [margin] of the world, and not after Christ."[40]

Seeing, then, that the Platonic system of education has exerted, and is still exerting, such an influence over the minds of men, it behooves us to ascertain the basic principles of his system. What did the man believe, and what did he teach? Quotations have already been given showing that he is the father of *modern philosophy*. Emerson defines this philosophy. He says: *"Philosophy is the account which the human mind, gives to itself of the constitution of the world."* All attempts, then, to account for the constitution of the world when a "thus saith the Lord," is refused, is philosophy. And philosophy is Plato.

"Through faith we understand that the worlds were framed by the word of God, so that things which are seen were not made of things which do appear."[41] But Platonism is the *mind* trying to account to itself for the constitution of the worlds. How, think you, did the author of this philosophy go about to account for things which can be grasped by *faith alone?* "To Plato belongs the honor of first subjecting education to a scientific examination," says Painter. Here began the laboratory studies which have been continued by Huxley, Darwin, and others. And thus, from Plato, Europe and America have gained their ideas of evolution. Plato brought these ideas from Egypt and Babylon, and the schools of today follow this man-made philosophy. Our men of intellect write text-books which they place in the hands of youth, teaching them to account for the constitution of the worlds according to the reasoning of men's minds.

A few more thoughts concerning Plato, and we shall see what evolution is, and where it is now found. Aristotle, the illustrious pupil of Plato, "created the science of logic," "the science of *exact* reasoning," as Webster puts it. Says Emerson: "The balanced soul came." "His daring imagination gives him the more solid grasp of facts....According to the old sentence, 'If Jove should descend to the earth, *he would speak in the style of Plato.*' " This last, the Christian can readily believe; but the Son of man used an entirely different speech, although Plato antedates his birth over four hundred years, and was, at the time of the advent of Christ, the ruler of the intellectual world.

"In reading logarithms, one is not more secure than following Plato in his flights." Plato himself is given credit for saying: "There is a science of sciences—I call it Dialectic—*which is the intellect discriminating the false and the true.*" There is indeed a science of sciences—the science of salvation. There is verily a way of judging between the false and the true, for the Spirit of truth will guide you into all truth. But the human brain can never do this. It was this same logic, Plato's "science of sciences," which was given such prominence in the papal schools and all medieval education.

Here stand the two systems side by side, the one guided by human reason, the other by the Spirit of the living God. Remember that the world bows to Plato; and, raising its hands in an attitude of worship, lays at his feet its tribute, its dearest idol—its educational system. Chambers's Encyclopedia, art. "Plato," shows conclusively that this Greek philosopher holds still his exalted position in literary circles and among educators. It says: "Since the French Revolution particularly, the study of Plato has been pursued with renewed vigor in Germany, France, and England; and many of our distinguished authors, without expressly professing

Platonism—as Coleridge, Wordsworth, Mrs. Browning, Ruskin, etc.—have formed a strong and growing party of adherents, who *could find no common banner under which they could at once so conveniently and so honorably muster as that of Plato.*"

Christians are to be gathered under the ensign of Christ;[42] but many educators of today find "no common banner under which they could so conveniently and so honorably muster as that of Plato." Christianity or paganism, which shall it be in the education of Protestant children of today? How did it happen that the ideas of Plato were so generally accepted throughout Europe? The article in Chambers's Encyclopedia, from which the foregoing quotation is made, tells in the following words how the early Christian church became contaminated by the teachings of Plato: "The works of Plato were extensively *studied by the church fathers*, one of whom joyfully recognizes, in the great teacher of the academy, the schoolmaster who, in the fullness of time, was destined to educate the heathen for Christ, as Moses did the Jews." If the early church adopted the educational system of Plato, one does not wonder that by the Middle Ages Europe was ready for Greek philosophy.

In the year 1453, the Turks captured Constantinople, and "many Greek scholars took refuge in Italy. The times were propitious for them." Let it be remembered that this was one of the mileposts in the history of the Dark Ages. The Latin tongue had been the universal language during the days of papal supremacy. There was an uprising against the tyranny of the papacy over thought, and the modern tongues began to appear. In order to stem the tide without losing ground, the papacy turned the attention of men's minds to Greek classics rather than to the Bible of Wycliffe or Erasmus, and a little later to the writings of Luther. Indeed, for the papacy the "times were propitious."

"Noble and wealthy patronage was not lacking, and under its fostering care they (the Greeks) became for a time the teachers of Europe. *They succeeded in kindling a remarkable enthusiasm for antiquity.* Manuscripts were collected, translations were made, *academies were established,* and libraries were founded. Several of the popes became generous patrons of ancient learning....Eager scholars from England, France, and Germany sat at the feet of Italian masters, in order afterward to bear beyond the Alps the precious seed of the new culture."[43] Painter further gives the effects of this spread of Greek classics: "In Italy it tended strongly to *paganize* its adherents. Ardor for antiquity became at last intoxication. Infidelity prevailed in the highest ranks of the church; Christianity was despised as a superstition; immorality abounded in the most shameful forms. The heathenism of Athens was revived in Christian Rome." And scholars from England, France, and Germany sat at the feet of these heathen teachers, drinking in their philosophy, and then hastening across the Alps to propagate these ideas in the schools for the education of the young. This was the influence against which the Reformation had to fight. It is from Oxford, Cambridge, and the universities of Germany and France that American colleges and universities have imbibed these same pagan ideas.

The classics form the backbone of paganism, as *the Bible forms the basis of Christian education.* The classics are enduring, because they are the highest product of the human mind. The recent move in educational circles, and on the part of some of our leading colleges against the study of the "humanities" (the Greek and Latin classics), and in favor of the study of "moderns" (that is, science, modern languages, and history), can never reach a point of stability until the Bible is put in its proper position as an educational factor, for to push out the classics without putting in their place that which is equally as strong, *if not stronger,* is useless. A reaction is inevitable, and the classics will be returned to their old-time place of honor. Christian education in its simplicity is the only alternative.

This does not mean the substitution of a class in Bible or sacred history for the former classics. As the classic literature has been the basis of all instruction in our schools since the Middle Ages, a reformation necessitates a decided breaking down of the old system, and the adoption of a new system built upon an entirely different foundation—a system in which the Word of God shall be the basis of all education, and the text-book in every line of study.

Parents, reading this, may say that but a small proportion of the people ever obtain a classical education. But if you send your child only to the modern kindergarten, he is there told the story of Pluto; or of Ceres, goddess of the golden grain; Mercury, the winged messenger god; the wood nymphs; Aeolus, who rules the winds and brings the storms; or Apollo, who is driven across the heavens in a chariot of fire. Or, if the real Greek names are dropped, *nature is personified* in such a way as to give the childish mind a distorted idea of things which leads to anything but the pure and simple truth of God's Word. He thus drinks in the myths and fables of the Greeks from very infancy. One of his First Readers has the story of Proserpina, who was stolen, and hidden under the earth for a season. Nature-studies are often made attractive to youthful minds by being associated with the ancient Greek gods and goddesses. But even in a more subtle way the ideas of classic lore are taught in the evolutionary theories of science and philosophy, through primary, grammar, and high school grades.

"Philosophy," as before quoted, is defined to be "the account which the human mind gives to itself of the constitution of the world." That philosophy is now termed *evolution*, for evolution is man's way of accounting for the constitution of the world, and the creatures which inhabit it. Take notice of these words from the pen of Henry Drummond. In a paper prepared for the Parliament of Religions, entitled "Evolution of Christianity," he says: "Working in its own field, science made the discovery of *how God made the world.*" "Through faith *we* understand that the worlds were framed by the word of God," writes Paul to the Hebrews.[44]

Mr. Drummond continues: "To science itself this discovery was startling and as unexpected as it has ever been to theology. Exactly fifty years ago Mr. Darwin wrote in dismay to Mr. Hooker that the old theory of *specific creation*—that God made all species apart, and introduced them into the world one by one—was melting away before his eyes. He unburdened the thought, as he says in his letter, almost as if he were confessing a murder. But *so entirely has the world bowed to the weight of facts before which* even Darwin trembled, that one of the last books on Darwinism by so religious a mind as that of Mr. Alfred Russell Wallace, contains in its opening chapter these words: 'The whole scientific and literary world, *even the whole educated public, accepts as a matter of common knowledge the origin of the species from the other allied species,* by the ordinary process of natural birth. *The idea of special creation, or any other exceptional mode of production, is absolutely extinct.*' "

It would be well if each could read the words of Drummond for himself; but in brief he says: "It is needless at this time of day to point out the surpassing grandeur of the new conception [evolution]. How it has filled the Christian imagination and kindled to enthusiasm the soberest scientific minds from Darwin downward is known to everyone. For that *splendid hypothesis we cannot be too grateful to science;* and that theology can only enrich itself which gives it even temporary place in its doctrine of creation."

How strange that God failed to make known this stupendous truth (?) through his Word, and left it for science in the hands of Plato's descendants to figure out! "What it needed," says Drummond, "was a credible presentation, in view especially of astronomy, geology, paleontology, and biology. These, as we have said, had made the former theory simply untenable. *And science has supplied theology with a theory which the intellect can accept.*" Faith has been laid aside. The human intellect has been exalted, Paganism has cast out Christianity, and our boys and girls now study the nebular hypothesis, explanatory of the creation of the worlds, in their astronomy and geography; they dwell upon the eons of ages consumed in the formation of the geologic strata of the earth; they study the fossils of the ages past, and from them describe the evolution of man from a polyp.

Of what use is the preaching of the gospel on one day of the week, while six days out of seven paganism guides the intellect? Why sit dreaming of heaven, or spend money to proselyte, while pagan education leads your own children by the hand, and weaves about their mind a network of theories which blinds their eyes to spiritual truths? There is weight in the words of President Harper, of Chicago University, who says, "It is difficult to prophesy what the result of our present method of educating the youth will be in fifty years. We are training the mind in our public schools, but the moral side of the child's nature is almost entirely neglected. The Roman Catholic Church insists on remedying this manifest evil, but our Protestant churches seem to ignore it completely. They expect the Sunday-school to make good what our public schools leave undone, and the consequence is that we overlook a danger as real and as great as any we have had to face."

Chapter VIII
Christ the Educator of Educators

I. The Christ Life

To Israel as a nation had been entrusted the sacred gift of teaching; but the power had departed from this people because they had mingled their educational ideas with the heathen, and had so far forgotten the commands of Jehovah that they were sending their children to heathen teachers, inviting into their midst the prophets of Baal.45 That nation whose prophets had more than once warned the kings of the earth of impending danger, heard no longer the voice of God. For nearly four hundred years no prophet had arisen in Israel. "Prophecy had become so completely extinct— the Spirit had so utterly departed from Israel—that it was apparently assumed by many that a new prophet was an impossibility." Had the God who brought their fathers out of Egypt, who had driven out the nations before their face— the God of Abraham, Isaac, and Jacob—had He forsaken His people? Often the question was asked, as the family circle formed around the table. Almost with bated breath mothers awaited the birth of a child, hoping it might be the chosen of God, but still no prophet came.

The priests in Israel went on in their formal round of duties; yearly the nation assembled at Jerusalem for the annual feasts. Thousands of victims were slain, and the blood ran freely from the altar; but there was no answering fire, no glow of the Shekinah. Jewish children sat day after day at the feet of masters in Israel, listening to the repetition of tradition and the words of the Talmud; but the life had departed from the instruction, and there was no response in the souls of men. Heaven waited anxiously for the opening of some soul to the inflow of God's Spirit, but the avenues through which it should have come were closed. Teachers who should have been "under the full control of the Spirit," knew not what it was to hear the voice of God; and children, fed only with physical and mental food, grew to manhood with shriveled spiritual natures, to become in turn the teachers of the next generation. As Israel's governmental prosperity was due to her educational system, as her land produced abundantly when the children were properly taught, and as the nations round them bowed in respect to the chosen of God so long as they adhered to the system of education once offered, it is no wonder that the year 5 B. C., following centuries of departure from these truths, found Palestine in the iron grasp of Rome, and its people scarce able to pay the necessary tribute. Heaven's eye saw this and more.

Among the priests who ministered in the temple was one who looked for a deliverer, and to him the angel Gabriel came with the words: "Thy prayer is heard; and thy wife Elizabeth shall bear thee a son, and thou shalt call his name John." Although this man had touched the chord on which angels sang, and was enabled to feel the pulse-beat of the Eternal; the angel's words startled him, and he believed them not. And that the sounds of earth might for a time be shut out, and Zacharias be enabled to listen only to the voice of God, the angel laid his hand upon him, and he remained speechless until the day of the fulfillment of Gabriel's words.

A prophet was born who was to turn the hearts of Israel to their God. He came in the spirit and power of Elias; preaching repentance. His life was one of loneliness and poverty. His time was spent away from the cities and multitudes; for Jerusalem, the appointed leader of nations, no longer offered an education fitted for her own prophets. And so, God trained John. Of those born of women there is none greater than John the Baptist.

Once more heaven and earth were linked., How small the chain! Only, as it were, the size of a thread, and the connecting link was the heart of a woman! But in the town of Nazareth, the lowly and the despised, lived a young woman, betrothed to Joseph, a carpenter of Galilee. Looking into the future, little more than dreaming of life and its hopes, she lifted her eyes, and beheld an angel. The soul longing to be in tune with God, brings angelic hosts to earth. If that yearning be but a mother's longing, heaven bows a listening ear; the throb is felt throughout creation. So close is God to man! The words, "Hail, highly favored, the Lord is with thee;" startled Mary, for she had not expected such a quick response. She was troubled, but the angel said, "Fear not, Mary." "The power of the Highest shall overshadow thee; therefore, also, that holy thing which shall be born of thee shall be called the Son of God." "The fullness of time had come." God, having waited years for Israel to return to Him, now accomplished the master stroke of the Godhead. Creation wondered.

The Spirit overshadowed Mary; it thrilled her nerves, and touched to life the germ of a new being. To humanity was given the power to form a body for the indwelling of the God of heaven. "A body hast Thou prepared Me." The treasure was in an earthen vessel, that the more glory might abound to God. "Christ set up His tabernacle in the midst of our human encampment. He pitched His tent by the side of the tents of men, that He might dwell among us, and make us familiar with His divine character and life."[46]

The early years of the Christ child found Him sitting *at His mother's knee.* From her lips and from the *scrolls of the prophets,* He learned of heavenly things! *Nature* was His unwearied teacher; from her He gathered stores of scientific knowledge. He studied the life of plants and animals, and the life of man." "The parables by which, during His ministry, He loved to teach His lessons of truth, show how open His spirit was to the influences of nature, and how He had gathered the spiritual teaching from the surroundings of His daily life." "As the hart panteth after the water brooks," so panted His soul for spiritual intercourse with the Father; and that longing which led Him to listen attentively for the voice of God in nature, developed the highest powers of His mind.

His was not a sudden growth, but gradual, as with other children; and while developing a strong physical body, "the child grew, and waxed strong in spirit, filled with wisdom." The secret of the difference between Jesus and His companions is revealed in this verse. Most children develop mentally and physically, especially during their first twelve years; but the spiritual nature of Christ was the leading one and in His threefold nature the mental and physical were always well balanced by the spiritual. As Hinsdale says: "The divine mind, the human heart, and nature are closely united" in Him. *He did not seek instruction in the rabbinical schools, for they had lost the spirit which to him was life.*

At an early age, probably not later than twelve, He recognized His life work, and henceforth every energy was bent in one direction. His lot was to reveal the divinity of God, to show the possibilities of the God-man, to prove to the world that it is possible for God and man to unite and for the spiritual nature to rule; and proving this, to show that the heavenly instituted system of education was not a failure, although at that time it was in disrepute.

The age of twelve was a critical period in the life of a Jewish child, for it was then that the physical nature was approaching maturity. The next few years meant much to the youth, for he then had it within his power to choose for life the plane upon which he expected to live. If physical strength and the gratification of the natural senses are the height of ambition, by yielding to temptations of this nature at about this age the life-habits are fixed. Perhaps in other countries the development is somewhat slower, owing to climatic influences, but from twelve to sixteen every youth struggles against tendencies and ambitions which a few years later cease to be temptations. It was so with Christ; but as He stood watching the paschal services at the time of His first visit to the temple, "day by day He saw their meaning more clearly. Every act seemed to be bound up with His own life. New impulses were awakening within

Him." For years, that service, established to appeal to the spiritual nature, had degenerated into the mere slaying of beasts. For the first time a soul was touched, and heavenly impulses were awakened. It was then that the temptation to pass a life in physical ease was met and overcome. Heaven seemed to open to the child's eyes, and He heard the call of God to a life with Him. He sought to be alone, and in the silence His heart caught the vibrations of heavenly beings, and the grosser physical nature was abandoned forever.

The resolve formed, a new light and power seemed to take possession of His mind, and entering the school conducted in the temple, He listened eagerly to hear from the lips of the rabbis some spiritual lesson. "The doctors turned upon Him with questions, and they were amazed at His answers." He manifested such deep piety, and His questions opened to the minds of His listeners such depths of truth, that wonder filled their minds. A harp swept by heavenly zephyrs was before them, and the music fell on untrained ears. *The first work of the heaven-sent teacher had begun.* "Wist ye not that I must be about My Father's business?" He asked, as Joseph and Mary met Him at the temple gate. They saw Him with physical eyes, and thought Him all their own; but the eye of the child had pierced the cloud which hung between heaven and earth.

From Jerusalem He returned with His parents, and aided them in their life of toil. "He hid in His own heart the mystery of His mission, waiting submissively for the appointed time for Him to enter upon His work." Those eighteen years were years of toil and study. Each day drew Him nearer to the time when a voice from heaven should proclaim Him a divine teacher.

He was not impatient, but as a carpenter did thorough work; as a son, He was obedient; and as a subject, He was law-abiding.

He never lost sight of the fact that He had a mission, and that it took a spiritual life to fulfill that mission. He was tempted in all points, and suffered in the temptation;

but each resistance was a round added in the ladder He was building toward heaven. There was a law in Israel calling the priests to their sacred office at the age of thirty. This statute was based upon a law of human nature. The allotted time of man's life is divided into two portions. The first forty years is a time of growth, the last thirty a period of decline. Of the first half we have the age of physical development, then a time when the intellectual powers are in the ascendancy, and from twenty- five to thirty or thirty-five is the time of special development in the spiritual nature. Every man has three chances in life; and the choice made, whether for worldly honor, for intellectual powers, or a life of faith, *depends wholly upon the object constantly kept before the child by its educators.* Had Christ been under the influence of the teachers of His day, the probability is that He would have chosen to live either on the physical or the intellectual plane, for this was the choice made by all the pupils of those schools, but His early training by Mary, who, as a mother, had yielded herself as the "handmaid of the Lord," and His close communion with God through the works of nature, guided Him into right channels, and at the auspicious moment He voluntarily offered Himself to His Father to fulfill the mission which it lay in His power to reject. Of His later struggles the record is silent. There came a period, however, when He might have posed as an intellectual leader, but His earlier decision led Him to pass this temptation unsullied. To prove this true, we need only to study the nature of the temptations presented in the wilderness. That He remained true to His mission is due to early training. This will not be controverted, for it is a divine law seen everywhere in nature.[47]

II. The Ministry of the God-Man

One of the gifts of the Spirit is that of teaching, and Christ was a born teacher. Acquired ability amounts to but little where the spirit of teaching is wanting. Christ was a teacher both by virtue of His nationality, since all Jews were called to be teachers, and also by direct appointment; for He had to accomplish in His own life what the nation had refused to accomplish.

He carried with Him no credentials, no statement of scholarship signed by the doctors of Israel, for none of these schools had known Him as a pupil; yet Nicodemus, a master teacher in Jerusalem, after listening to His words, sought Him in the quiet evening hours, and addressed Him as *Rabbi*—Teacher. In the course of the conversation this learned man said, "We know that thou art a divine teacher, for no man can do as Thou except God be with him." It was as a teacher, and more, as a divine teacher, that He was known from the very beginning of His ministry. His ministry was a ministry of *teaching*. He was known as a teacher, not so much by the words He spoke as *by the life He lived*, and the works He did.

The words of Bushnell are true: "We can see for ourselves in the simple directions and freedom of His teachings, that whatever He advances is from Himself." He was giving Himself, and that He had a self, a divine self, to give is *due to the education of the child and youth*. God's image was perfect in Him, and when the time of ministry came, there shone from Him what previous years had been developing in Him. This is the object of Christian education. The same author further says: "He is the high-priest…of the divine nature, speaking as one that has come out from God, *and has nothing to borrow from the world*. It is not to be detected…that the *human sphere in which He moved imparted anything to Him*. His teachings are just as full of divine nature, as Shakespeare's of human." What a commentary on the two systems of education, the one choosing *inspiration* as a basis; the other, the product of the human brain!

Bushnell continues: "In His teaching He does not speculate about God, as a school professor, drawing out conclusions by a practice on words, and deeming that the way of

proof; He does not build up a frame of evidence from below, by some constructive process, such as the philosophers
delight in; but He simply speaks of God and spiritual things
as one who has come out from Him, *to tell us what He
knows*. And His simple telling brings us the reality; proves
it to us in its own sublime self-evidence; awakens even the
consciousness of it in our own bosom; so that formal arguments or dialectic proofs *offend us by their coldness*, and
seem, in fact, to be only opaque substances set between us
and the light. Indeed, He makes even the world luminous
by His words—fills it with an immediate and new sense
of God, which nothing has ever been able to expel. The
incense of the upper world is brought out in His garments,
and flows abroad, as perfume, on the poisoned air." And no
wonder, for from a child He had breathed the atmosphere
of heaven. *Every child should have the same privilege.*

When the two teachers, Christ and Nicodemus, the representatives of two systems of education, the divine and the
worldly, met, Christ outlined to his questioner the principles upon which His system was based:[48]

–Its primary object is to prepare its pupils for the
kingdom of God, a spiritual kingdom.

–The first step is a spiritual birth; for "God is a Spirit:
and they that worship Him must worship in spirit." "That
which is born of the flesh is flesh; and that which is born
of the Spirit is spirit."

–This the natural man cannot understand, for it is
spiritually discerned. As well might I try to explain it to
you, Nicodemus, as to explain the blowing of the winds;
you can see the results, but the truth cannot be grasped by
the senses. Do you pose as a teacher in Israel, and know
not these things? "If I have told you earthly things, and ye
believe not, how shall ye believe, if I tell you of heavenly
things?" I have but begun to tell you of the plan of the Father. There are yet many things, "but ye cannot bear them
now."

–The things I teach are as light in the darkness. "Every one that doeth evil hateth the light,… but he that doeth truth cometh to the light." It is thus that I distinguish true scholars from the false. When truth is offered, some believe, and whosoever believes in the Son of man shall have eternal life.

Nicodemus said "How *can* these things be?" He longed for proof, for demonstration. "*Proof* is indeed the method of science, including theology; it has, no doubt, a function in religious teaching; but *it is not the method of the highest form of religious teaching.* The fundamental truths of religion are directly revealed to the human consciousness, and are not argued out or logically established. *The greatest religious truths lie deeper than formal reasoning.* This is the reason why *the greatest religious teachers have worked below the proposition-and-proof level;* as said before, they have something of the prophetic gift. It may be added that no preacher [or teacher] who works mainly on this line will attract the most religious minds; he will not attract even those who have the piety of the intellect, to say nothing of the piety of the affections and the will. He may develop logical acumen, critical ability, and controversial power, but he will prove unequal to the generation of spirituality.... Such a minister will be sure to lead his flock into the error that is now far too common—of assigning a disproportionate place in religious faith and life to the understanding, to the partial exclusion of the heart."[49]

His actual work as a teacher is seen in His dealings, first, with the apostles, His immediate followers, who were in training that they in turn might become teachers; second, with the multitudes who thronged His way; third, with the children who were brought to Him by mothers, and who were taught by Him, that mothers and apostles might the better know how to deal with youthful minds. Primarily, His was a training-school for workers, and His pupils represented every phase of human disposition. He chose humble fishermen, because their minds were unprejudiced, and they had less to unlearn before accepting the truth. "He knew what was in man." That is, He had insight into the minds and hearts, and knew just what was needed to awaken the soul-life of each student. This is a necessary gift in the successful teacher. How much that is now taught would be dispensed with if teachers could read the soul conditions of pupils, and then feed them with only such food as would nourish. *This, too, is Christian education.* Before the teacher can have such an experience, however, he must have soul culture, and be in such close touch with the fountain of truth that he can draw whatever is needed. The well is deep, and *faith alone can bring the water of life to the surface.*[50]

With His chosen apostles, Christ *"withdrew from the confusion of the city to the quiet of the fields and hills* as more in harmony with the lessons of self-abnegation he desired to teach them. Here, surrounded by the works of his own creation, he could turn the thoughts of his hearers *from the artificial to the natural."* Those schools today which are located in some quiet country place afford the best opportunities for education.

The books used seem to be two, and only two: *the writings of the prophets and the great book of nature.* Hinsdale says: "Scripture furnishes the basis of His teaching. It is impossible to say how many distinct recognitions of Scripture are found in His teachings, but the number and range are both large. One of the most interesting of these [methods] is his constant habit of expanding Scripture, or, as we might say, of reading into it, new meanings. He thus treats not merely prophetic passages, but also dogmatic passages; moreover, His meanings are sometimes new, not merely to the Jewish teachers, but also to the authors of the passages themselves."[51] This was because the teacher was led by the Spirit of truth, which guides into all truth.

It must be remembered that this instruction was given to men of mature minds, and tended to fit them to become teachers of all men in whatever station. Probably none of the apostles were under thirty. They were men who had become settled in a life work. John, the youngest, was most susceptible to spiritual teaching, and at length developed this nature so fully that his spirit left his body in vision.[52] Painter expresses well the method of instruction followed by Christ. He says: "He observes the order of nature, and seeks only a gradual development—'first the blade, then the ear, after that the full corn in the ear.' With His disciples, He insists chiefly upon the *practical* and *fundamental* truths of religion, *building*, as it were, a substantial framework in the beginning, which the Holy Spirit was to conduct afterward to a harmonious and beautiful completion."[53]

It was thus that all the truths we call doctrines were taught. The lesson on the resurrection was at the tomb of Lazarus; the one on Sabbath observance was in the synagogue, healing the withered hand, or bidding the dumb to speak. "One finds in His program," says a French writer, "neither literary studies nor course of theology. And yet, strange as it may seem, when the moment of action arrives, the disciples—those unlettered fishermen—have become orators that move the multitudes and confound the doctors; profound thinkers that have sounded the Scriptures and the human heart; writers that give to the world immortal books in a language not their mother tongue." If the worth of a system of education is to be judged by results, the world must hold its peace when looking upon the work of Christ.

Astonishment will again take hold of men when Christians return to His methods. Of His reference to nature we have no need to write, for His parables are the wonder of the ages, and take a unique position in the literature of all times. Christ was not, as many other teachers, a writer of books. His writing was on the hearts of men. He spoke, and the vibratory waves set in motion have continued until today, and still beat upon our hearts. The soul of the spiritually minded hears, and men today become pupils of the Man of Nazareth as verily as did Peter, James, and John.

A student was ready to go forth from Christ's teachings to open the truth to others only when he could say, "Lo, now speakest Thou plainly....Now we are sure that Thou knowest all things, and needest not that any man should ask Thee. By this we believe that Thou camest forth from God."[54] With the multitudes He did a work similar to that with the disciples; but because they were coming and going, He could not do the same thorough work. His teaching, however, was *always practical*, and the farmer went to his field a better man, seeing God in the growing grain; the fisherman returned to his nets with the thought ringing in his mind that he should be a fisher of men; the mother returned to her home recognizing her children as younger members of God's family, and with a strong desire to teach as He taught.

The tendency always in all His teaching was to arouse thought, to awaken soul-longings, and cause hearts to beat with a new life fed from above.

Standing between heaven and earth of the musical scale, His life vibrated in unison with those higher notes of the universes circling round His Father's throne, and with His human arm He encircled the world, imparting to beings here the same life, striving always to bring them into tune with the Infinite. "I, if I be lifted up," He said, "will draw all men unto Me."

Chapter IX
Education in the Early Church

I PRAY not that Thou shouldest take them out of the world, but that Thou shouldest keep them from the evil. They are not of the world, even as I am not of the world. Sanctify [teach] them through Thy truth."55 As He lifted His eyes to heaven in those moments of quiet, just before entering Gethsemane, these words fell from the lips of the Son of man. Looking upon the little company of men clustering around Him, He saw in them the nucleus of the church which was to be called by His name, and His heart yearned for that body of Christians. Many and fierce would be their struggles; for He had breathed into the hearts of men a system of instruction which, because it was truth, would awaken all the bitterness of the enemy of truth; and the new system must be able to resist all the darts which human minds, swayed by the prince of evil, could hurl. Divine philosophy must meet and vanquish human philosophy. That was now the controversy, and it was left to a few weak men to start the work. What power was in that Spirit of truth with which they were baptized! His commission to this same company, as they watched Him recede from earth on the day of His ascension, was, "Go ye therefore, and teach all nations." They, the true Israel, were now to become teachers of nations.

Recognizing the difficulties to be met, He had, on another occasion, said: "I send you forth as sheep among wolves: be ye therefore wise as serpents, and simple as doves." In no boasted philosophy, no high-sounding words, but *in simplicity of truth, was to lie their strength.* Of the works of the apostles and those who believed on Christ through their teaching, we have this divine testimony, "I know thy works, and thy labor, and thy patience, and how thou canst not bear them which are evil: and thou hast tried them which say they are apostles, and are not, and hast found them liars: and hast borne, and hast patience, and for my name's sake hast labored and hast not fainted."[56] It is therefore evident that a great work was done, and that very speedily; for again Inspiration describes it: "Behold a white horse: and he that sat on him had a bow;...and he went forth conquering, and to conquer."[57] Men, though admonished to be as harmless as doves, were nevertheless, when teachers of truth, enabled to make themselves felt in the world.

To accept Christianity in those early days meant the withdrawal from everything before cherished; it meant not only the separation from heathenism in worship, or Babylon, but also *from heathenism in thought* and education, or *Egypt*. It was a second exodus. Justin Martyr, a Christian born near the close of the first century, is quoted by Painter, as he describes the life of a follower of Christ: "We who once delighted in lewdness now embrace chastity; we who once embraced magical arts, have consecrated ourselves to the good and unbegotten God; we who loved above all things the gain of money and possessions, now bring all that we have into one common stock, and give a portion to everyone that needs; we who once hated and killed one another, now pray for our enemies."

With this spirit in the church we are not surprised to find that in the words of Coleman, *"The tender solicitude of these early Christians for the religious instruction of their children is one of their most beautiful characteristics.* They taught them, even at the earliest dawn of intelligence, the sacred names of God and the Savior. They sought to lead the infant minds of their children up to God, by familiar narratives from Scripture, of Joseph, of young Samuel, of Josiah, and of the holy child Jesus. The history of the patriarchs and prophets, apostles, and men whose lives are narrated in the sacred volume, *were the nursery tales* with which they sought to form the tender minds of their children. As the mind of the child expanded, the parents made it their sacred duty and delightful task daily to exercise him in the recital of select passages of Scripture relating to the doctrines and duties of religion. The Bible was the entertainment of the fireside. *It was the first, the last, the only schoolbook almost, of the child;* and sacred psalmody, the only song with which his infant cry was hushed as he was lulled to rest on his mother's arm. The sacred song and the rude melody of its music were, from the earliest periods of Christian antiquity, an important means of impressing the infant heart with sentiments of piety, and of imbuing the susceptible minds of the young with the knowledge and the faith of the Scriptures."

Painter writes: The purpose of these early Christian parents, as of the ancient Jews, was to train up their children in the fear of God. In order that the children might be exposed as little as possible to the corrupting influence of heathen associations, *their education was conducted within the healthful precincts of home.* As a result, they grew up without a taste for debasing pleasures; they acquired simple domestic tastes; and when the time came, they took their place as consistent and earnest workers in the church."[58] These words make several facts very prominent:

1. Christian education should begin in the home.

2. Bible stories should be the basis for nursery tales and infant songs.

3. Christians should carry out the plan of education which the Jews failed to obey, and which Christ revealed in a new light.

4. The results of such Christian education in the home school will be elevated characters and workers in the cause of God.

Would that it could be said of Christian mothers today, as a heathen orator once exclaimed concerning those early followers of Christ, "What wives these Christians have!"

One of the early fathers thus expresses the danger of children and youth in the schools of the world, and shows the character of the education needed: "Mothers ought to care for the bodies of their children, but it is necessary also that they inspire their offspring with love for the good and with fear toward God. And fathers will not limit themselves to giving their children an earthly vocation, but will interest themselves also in their heavenly calling.

"The most beautiful heritage that can be given children is to teach them to govern their passions....Let us have for our children the same fear that we have for our houses, when servants go with a light into places where there is inflammable material, as hay or straw. They should not be permitted to go where the fire of impurity may be kindled in their hearts, and do them an irreparable injury. A knowledge of the Scriptures is an antidote against the unreasonable inclinations of youth and against the reading of pagan authors, in which heroes, the slaves of every passion, are lauded. *The lessons of the Bible are springs that water the soul.* As our children are everywhere surrounded by bad examples, the monastic schools [what would correspond today with church schools] are the best for their education. *Bad habits once contracted, they cannot be got rid of.* This is the reason God conducted Israel into the wilderness... that the vices of the Egyptians might be unlearned....Now our children are surrounded by vice in our cities and are unable there to resist bad examples....*Let us take care of the souls of our children,* that they may be formed for virtue, and not be degraded by vice."

This writer might well address a modern audience, for he recognizes the influence of pagan authors, and states that the Bible alone can counteract this influence; *he recognizes the worldly schools as Egypt,* and says that Christians should take their children out; and finally, he recognizes the value of having schools located in the country, and advises people to move out of the cities with their children.

Mosheim says: "There can be no doubt but that the children of Christians were carefully trained up from their infancy, and were early put to reading the sacred books and learning the principles of religion. For this purpose, *schools* were erected everywhere from the beginning."[59]

From these schools for children, we must distinguish those *seminaries* of the early Christians, erected extensively in the larger cities, at which adults, and especially *such as aspired to be public teachers*, were instructed and educated in all branches of learning, both human and divine. Such seminaries, in which young men devoted to the sacred office were taught whatever was necessary to qualify them properly for it, the apostles of Christ undoubtedly both set up themselves, and directed others to set up.[60] St. John at Ephesus, and Polycarp at Smyrna, established such schools. Among these seminaries, in subsequent times, none was more celebrated than that at Alexandria; which is commonly called a catechetic school."[61]

In addition, then, to home and church schools for children, the early Christian church established seminaries for the education of workers. In reading the history of the times the course of instruction is seen to adhere closely to the Scriptures, and to draw a sharp distinction between the science of salvation and the Greek and Oriental philosophy as taught in the pagan schools.

Christian education was often regarded as narrow and limited by those who loved to study the mysteries of Greek wisdom; but as long as they adhered to their simple studies, and made faith the basis of their work, there was a power in the truths taught by the students of these schools, which made the pagan world, with all its great men, tremble. It is an interesting fact that as late as the fourth century, after the Christian schools had lost much of their power through the mingling of pagan with Christian methods, and the adoption of some of the pagan studies, they were still regarded as the stronghold of Christianity. When Julian, the apostate, began to reign, an attempt was made to revive paganism throughout the Roman Empire. One of his first acts was to *close the schools of the Christians.* "He contemptuously observes," says Gibbon, "that the men who exalt the merit of implicit faith are unfit to claim or to enjoy the advantages of science; and he vainly contends that if they refuse to adore the gods of Homer and Demosthenes, they ought to content themselves with expounding Luke and Matthew in the church of the Galileans.

"In all the cities of the Roman world, the education of the youth was entrusted to masters of grammar and rhetoric; who were *elected by the magistrates, maintained at the public expense,* and distinguished by many lucrative and honorable privileges....As soon as the resignation of the more obstinate teachers had established the unrivaled dominion of the pagan sophists, Julian invited the rising generation to resort with freedom to the *public schools,* in a just confidence that their tender minds would receive the impressions of *literature and idolatry.* If the greatest part of the Christian youth should be deterred by their own scruples, or by those of their parents, from accepting this dangerous mode of instruction, they must, at the same time, relinquish the benefits of a liberal education. Julian had reason to expect that, in the space of a few years, the church would relapse into its primeval simplicity, and that the theologians, who possessed an adequate share of the learning and eloquence of the age, would be succeeded by a generation of blind and ignorant fanatics, incapable of defending the truth of their own principles, or of exposing the various follies of polytheism."[62]

Julian cannot be counted as a fool; for, wishing to make the world pagan, he proceeded to do so, (1) *By closing the Christian schools where the "merit of implicit faith" was taught;* (2) *By compelling attendance of the public schools, taught by pagan teachers, and where literature and idolatry were combined.*

As Gibbon says, he had *just reason* to expect that in the course of a generation the Christians thus educated would lose their faith, cease to oppose paganism, and sink into insignificance. If a pagan emperor expected this in the fourth century, is it any wonder that Protestants today, allowing their children to remain in the public schools where precisely the same things are taught, in principle as Julian had his public instructors teach, should lose power and cease to be *Protestants*? From the words of Gibbon, one would infer that in the days of Julian there were parents who refused to send their children to the public schools; some children who, "because of their own, scruples," refused to attend; and some teachers who ceased to teach rather than teach literature and idolatry in state schools.

Special mention is made of the Alexandrian school, as it was located in an Egyptian city to which flocked many noted pagan scholars. Sad as it may be to do so, it is yet necessary to see how these schools, and especially this one at Alexandria, lost their simplicity as they came in contact with pagan scholars, and attempted to meet them on their own grounds.

Mosheim says: "This philosophy [of Plato] was adopted by such of the learned at Alexandria as wished to be accounted Christians, and *yet to retain the name, garb, and the rank of philosophers.* In particular, all those who in this century presided in the schools of the Christians at Alexandria... are said to have approved of it. These men were persuaded that true philosophy, the great and most salutary gift of God, lay in scattered fragments among all the sects of philosophers; and therefore, that it was the duty of every wise man, and especially of a Christian teacher, to collect those fragments from all quarters, and to use them for the defense of religion and the confutation of impiety."[63]

The lesson so dear to Paul—that the gospel of Christ is the "power of God unto salvation"—was lost sight of when these Christian teachers assumed the philosopher's garb, and used the philosopher's vocabulary to confute impiety.

"I have somewhat against thee," writes the divine historian of this age, "because thou hast left thy first love. Remember therefore from whence thou art fallen, and repent, and *do the first works*; or else I will come unto thee quickly, and will remove thy candlestick out of his place."[64] The heaven-lit taper of Christian education in its purity was beginning to grow dim. Its flame must have a constant supply of truth, or, like the candle without oxygen, it burns low, and finally goes out. Paul, writing to the Corinthians who were placed in circumstances similar to those of the school at Alexandria, that is, pressed upon all sides by pagan philosophy, said: "I came toward you with weakness and fear and great timidity. And my thought and my statement were not clothed in captivating philosophical reasons; but in demonstrated spirit and power, so that your trust might not be in *human philosophy*, but in divine power....What we speak is not in an artificial discussion of a human philosophy, but by spiritual teachings, comparing spiritualities with the spiritual."[65]

Again, "Dialectic," or logic, was that science of which Aristotle, the disciple of Plato, boasted as being the father. Says a writer of the church after the decline was well begun, it "is the queen of arts and sciences. *In it reason dwells,* and is manifested and developed. *It is dialectic alone that can give knowledge and wisdom;* it alone shows what and whence we are, and teaches us our destiny [human philosophy and evolution]; through it we learn to know good and evil. And *how necessary is it* to a clergyman, in order that he may be able to meet and vanquish heretics!" Men have more than once reverted to logic to vanquish heretics, but it was only when the Spirit of truth was lacking.

Error was rapidly creeping into the church, and it came principally through these schools, as has already been seen. However, truth was not abandoned for error without a struggle. Mosheim says: "The estimation in which human learning should be held was a question on which the Christians were about equally divided. For while many thought that the literature and writings of the Greeks ought to receive attention, *there were others who contended that true piety and religion were endangered by such studies.*[66] People then, as now, looked to the leaders in the church for guidance; and it was hard, when these studies were popular, for the conscientious to withdraw entirely to what the others called a narrow, limited education. It often led to contention among members of the same church, and often even parents and children failed to agree on the subject. "But gradually," continues Mosheim, "*the friends of philosophy and literature acquired the ascendancy.* To this issue Origen contributed very much; for having early imbibed the principles of the *new Platonism, he inauspiciously applied them to theology;* and earnestly recommended them to the numerous youth who attended on his instruction. And the greater the influence of this man, which quickly spread over the whole Christian world, the more readily was his method of explaining the sacred doctrines propagated."

The days when the papacy should be recognized as the beast of Revelation 13 were fast approaching. Such experiences in the history of education in the Christian church show how rapidly the life of the Master, the Spirit of truth, was giving place to the form of godliness which denied the power thereof. One reading thus the pages of history cannot fail to see that the papacy *was formed in the minds of men, was propagated in the schools, and really took birth in the educational system then developed.* The political power, which was called upon to help the church, simply carried out at the point of the sword those principles which were developed in the schools. The two streams—paganism and apostate Christianity—united; and in the mad current which flowed from their confluence, men's souls were lost forever.

Christian education is the pure water of life, clear and sparkling, which flows from the throne of God; but when mingled with the turbid waters of the valley, it is lost sight of, and the current is evil. The part played by Platonic philosophy cannot be overlooked. The foundation had already been laid in the third century for the scholasticism of the Middle Ages, and that "noontide of the papacy which was the world's moral midnight" was fast approaching.

Chapter X
The Papacy—
An Educational Problem

PREVIOUS chapters have revealed these facts: 1. That the Jewish nation was set as a light to the world. This light was to shine by means of education, and the Jews were to be teachers of the nations. 2. The Jewish nation lost its position as leader in educational reform, and, consequently, in all other particulars, because it departed from the pure system of education delivered to the fathers, and mingled with the heathen, especially with the Greeks and the Egyptians.

In substantiation of this fact we have these words of Neander: "The Jews, completely imbued with the elements of Hellenic culture, *endeavored to find a mean between it and the religion of their fathers*, which they had no wish to renounce. To this end they availed themselves of the system most in vogue with those who, in Alexandria, busied themselves with religious matters—that of the *Platonic philosophy*, which had already acquired a mighty influence over their own intellectual life....On the one hand, they firmly adhered to the religion of their fathers....On the other hand, their minds were possessed by a philosophical culture at variance with these convictions. They were themselves not unconscious of the conflicting elements that filled their minds, and must have felt constrained to seek some artificial method of combining them into a harmonious whole. Thus, they would be involuntarily driven to intercalate in *the old records of religion*, which for them possessed the highest authority, *a sense foreign to their true spirit*, supposing all the while that they were thereby really exalting their dignity as the source of all wisdom."⁶⁷ 3. *This intercalation of Greek philosophy* with the truth delivered to the Jewish nation brought the schools of the Hebrews to such a position that the Son of man, when receiving His education, avoided them altogether, and in His public teaching warned His people against the schools of the doctors, who for the Word of God taught the traditions of men. *This mingling of education then meant the crucifixion of Christ and the ruin of the Jewish nation.* 4. The early Christian church, composed of members called out from the Jewish schools and from the purely pagan doctrines, at first taught their children truths based upon the Scriptures; but before the close of the first century, the tendency to commingle Christian teachings and heathen philosophy was already noticeable. Paul, writing to the Thessalonians, referring to this fact, said, "The *mystery of iniquity* doth already work."

This tendency, seen in the days of Paul, grew into a habit; and as Christian youth prepared for gospel work by attending the schools at Alexandria and elsewhere, an entire change took place.

It now becomes our duty to follow this changed system of education, which is indeed but a mixture of Christian and pagan, and hence not a separate and distinct system at all. It was designated by the apostle to the Gentiles as "the mystery of iniquity." As found in the third century, Mosheim described it thus: "It is necessary, however, to observe that the methods now used of defending Christianity, and attacking Judaism and idolatry, degenerated much from the primitive simplicity, and the true rule of controversy. The *Christian doctors*, who had been *educated in the schools of the rhetoricians and sophists*, rashly employed the arts and evasions of their subtle masters in the service of Christianity; and, intent only upon defeating the enemy, they were too little attentive to the means of victory, indifferent whether they acquired it by artifice or plain dealing. This method of disputing, which the ancients called economical, and which *had victory for its object, rather than truth*, was, in consequence of the prevailing taste for rhetoric and sophistry, almost universally approved."[68]

The effect of the Christian schools' teaching Greek literature, sophistry, and rhetoric was bearing its fruit in an unmistakable way. The simplicity of the gospel and of the man of God, who was the *truth*, was fast passing away. Even at this early date we find the germ of the order of Jesuits, who, in the Middle Ages, carried out the theory of the Platonists, and asserted "that it was no sin for a person to employ falsehood and fallacies for the support of truth, when it was in danger of being borne down." It was at this time, and under the influence of these same doctors and teachers, that there arose the practice of attributing the writing of certain books to illustrious authors; "hence, the book of canons, which certain artful men ascribed falsely to the apostles,...and many other productions of that nature, which, for a long time, were too much esteemed by credulous men."[69] How far men had departed from the simplicity of the gospel is evident.

The spread of ideas contrary to the purity of the gospel was almost universally begun in the schools professing to be Christian; and teachers were, almost without exception, the leaders in these intellectual moves, which in reality form the basis for every change in government or religion. Throughout the history of the centuries, men have arisen who were noted for their intellectual prowess, men of strong mind, who were searching for truth. By tracing the work of a few representative teachers through the first three or four centuries, *we see the papacy appearing as the direct result of educational principles.*

In order to make this clear, let us begin with the teachings of Clement in the school of Alexandria. It may be hard to distinguish between truth and error, as we trace the intricate windings of philosophy in the days of the early

church; but it is necessary to find the origin of those leading principles of the papacy against which the Reformation
contended. In order to do so, we go to the source of the
stream, which is usually found at Alexandria, in the schools
conducted by Christian teachers, or doctors, as they are often called. The foremost, the all-absorbing doctrine of the
papacy, is the substitution of works for faith. Christ's one
lesson, illustrated in hundreds of ways, to the multitudes
and to the few, was wisdom by faith, eternal life by faith.
The early church was founded upon this principle, and faith
in God's Word was the first maxim in the home school, in
the church school, and in the seminaries of the early Christians. Faith gives the hearing ear, as in the case of Solomon;
this gives the ability to *study*, which brings true wisdom.

How or where faith was lost cannot be stated in positive terms. As wood, under favorable conditions, changes,
bit by bit, into solid stone, one atom of wood giving place
to a grain of sand, and so on till the form of the tree, once
an embodiment of life, now lies a hard and lifeless stone,
retaining, however, each scar of branch and leaf, each
crack or wrinkle of the bark, yea, even the annual marks of
growth and the grain of the wood; so faith in God's Word
was lost, atom by atom, and the lost faith was replaced by
human philosophy. Alexandria was to the Christian school
what the marsh is to the fallen tree. Much Greek philosophy contained elements of truth; many truths were by the
Greeks put in brilliant settings. God himself had evidently
revealed to the minds of men, such as Plato, Pythagoras,
Aristotle, and others, principles of truth; but it was not supposed that men to whom had been opened the treasures of
wisdom and knowledge through His word and through His
Son should ever find it necessary to search for a few gems
of truth amidst a mass of error. Turning from the pure light
to search for these stray thoughts in Greek philosophy, *men
lost their faith in God, failed to give His word its proper
place,* and erelong the living, fruit-bearing tree was but an
image of its former self, molded in stone.

That the reader may see that this mingling of truth and error was adopted in place of the pure word, he is referred to Neander's description of Clement and his quotations of that eminent scholar's reasoning.[70]

Without taking the space necessary to give this quotation, we pass to the thought that Clement introduced this Greek philosophy into the school he was teaching, and through his disciples paved the way for the papacy in its power. Of the Alexandrian school we read: "What was the original aim of the school itself? Was it at the outset merely an institution for communicating religious instruction to the heathen, or had there long existed in Alexandria a school for educating teachers for the Christian church—a sort of theological seminary for the clergy?...We find that originally a single person was appointed by the bishop of Alexandria to hold the office of catechist, whose business it was to give religious instruction to the heathen and probably *also to the children of the Christians in that place....* Men were required for this office who possessed a perfect acquaintance with the Grecian religion, and most especially must they have received a philosophical education, so as to be able to converse and to dispute with any learned pagans, who, after long investigation on other questions, might turn their attention to Christianity.

"*It was not enough to teach here, as in other churches, the main doctrines of Christianity....*With these enlightened catechumens, it was necessary to go back to the primitive sources of the religion in Scripture itself, and to seek to initiate them into the understanding of it—for such required a faith which would stand the *test of scientific examination.*"[71]

In order to meet the demands made by pagans and Greek philosophers the school stooped from its exalted position of teaching a wisdom acquired by faith, and substituted a course of study which "would *stand the test of scientific examination.*" Clement, one of the earliest teachers in this school, "points out the need of high and rich talents in the holder of the catechetical office at Alexandria." "The range of instruction imparted by these men," says Neander, "gradually extended itself, for they were the first who attempted to satisfy a want deeply felt by numbers—the want: of a *scientific exposition of the faith, and of a Christian science*." Here is perhaps the best place for one to attribute the change from faith to a scientific demonstration of the truths of the universe. Here is marked the time, so far as one is able to point it out with definiteness, of the transit from education by faith to education of the senses, from the spiritual to the intellectual and the physical. The fruit and the utter folly of the wisdom of the Greek and Egyptian sages (?) of this intellectual system are seen in its ripened state in the Dark Ages.

The same paragraph in Neander continues: "To their school were attracted not only those educated pagans, who, having by their teaching been converted to Christianity, and being seized with a desire to devote themselves and all they possessed to its service, chose... the Alexandrian catechists for their guides, but also *those youths*, who, having been brought up within the Christian pale, were thirsting after a more profound knowledge, in order to prepare themselves for the office of *church teachers*."[72]

This school did not find its pathway always strewn with roses; for there were church teachers of the primitive class "who looked chiefly to the practical and real... and who were in continual dread of a corruption of Christianity by the admixture of foreign philosophical elements", and these offered some opposition to the transit from an education of faith in God's Word to one of scientific investigation and reason.

Those were days of lively debate, and the defenders of Christian education more than once contended for its principles. " 'Thus much,' observes Clement, 'I would say to those who are so fond of complaining: if the philosophy is unprofitable, still the study of it is profitable, if any good is to be derived from thoroughly demonstrating that it is an unprofitable thing.' " This argument is indulged in at the present time by those who espouse the cause of modern education, and wish to defend the study of the classics and the doctrine of evolution.

The words of Clement in his arguments sound doubly striking, when we remember that today the feeling that the education of the senses will ultimately tend to the grasping of eternal truth by faith is just as firmly held as then, notwithstanding the fact that a careful investigation shows that this can never be the case, and that the only avenue to *truth* is through faith, first, last, and all the time. He says: "Perhaps the latter [philosophy] was given to the Greeks in a special sense, as preliminary to our Lord calling the Gentiles, since it educated them as the law did the Jews, for Christianity; and philosophy was a preparatory step for those who were to be conducted through Christ to perfection."[73]

Accordingly, we find Clement perpetually verging toward the gnostic or platonic position. "With an idea of faith which flowed from the very essence of Christianity, there was associated in his mind the still lingering notion, derived from the Platonic philosophy, of an opposition between a *religion of cultivated minds*, and arrived at by the medium of science, and a religion of the many, who were shackled by the senses and entangled in mere opinion."[74]

Here is distinctly seen the beginnings of that system of education which elevates the few and holds the masses in subjection. Herein lies the wellspring of a monarchical government and a papal hierarchy. It was the propagation of the system of education introduced into the Alexandrian school by Clement that formed the papacy. We are not surprised to read in history of the contest between the churches of Alexandria, Constantinople, and Rome. Rome as arbiter was called to decide between the Greek Catholics and the Alexandrians; and from the downfall of both her rivals she gained the pontifical throne; but it was only to crown the educational ideas of the Alexandrian school, and sway the world by the enforcement of the principles of that system of instruction *which substitutes scientific research for faith.* God had once called his people out of Egypt; but the church, forsaking the purity of the gospel, returned thither for its education. The Reformation was its second call, and today the third call is sounding. Having followed with some care the ideas first introduced by Clement, and finding that the result of the position taken by this teacher was that faith was destroyed and scientific reason substituted, we turn to the further development of this educational idea as advocated by one of Clement's most noted pupils and his successor in the Alexandrian school. I refer to Origen.

Origen was born 185 A. D., in Alexandria; he received a most liberal education, and was initiated at an early age into Hellenic science and art; the principles of Christianity were instilled into his mind by such teachers as Clement of Alexandria.[75] "He says himself that it was an outward motive that first led him to busy himself with the study of Platonic philosophy, and to make himself better acquainted generally with the systems of those who differed from himself. *The moving cause was his intercourse with heretics and pagans who had received a philosophical education.*"

"Attracted by his great reputation, such persons" came often to him, and he thus defends himself for bestowing his time on the Greek philosophy: "When I had wholly devoted my time to the promulgation of the divine doctrines, and the fame of my skill in them began to be spread abroad, so that both heretics and others, such as had been conversant with the Greek sciences, and particularly men from the philosophical schools, came to visit me, it *seemed to me necessary that I should examine the doctrinal opinions of the heretics, and what the philosophers pretended to know of the truth.*"[76]

These facts concerning Origen are given because the argument is strikingly similar to that used by many ministers and teachers of the present day, and because it shows how the Platonic philosophy gained such a foothold in so-called Christian schools, and grew into the papacy.

There are three individuals who stand as representatives of three systems of education. Plato personifies heathen philosophy; Christ said of Himself, "I am the… truth;" Origen personifies the mixture of the two—truth and error—and hence stands, from an educational standpoint, as *the father of the papacy*, which is the mystery of iniquity. It behooves us now to follow carefully the work of this man. After doing so, one can more readily understand why the beast is represented as having several heads."[77]

I quote extensively from Mosheim: "The principal doctrines of Christianity were now explained *to the people* in their native purity and simplicity, without any mixture of abstract reasonings or subtle inventions; nor were the feeble minds of the multitude loaded with a great variety of precepts. But the Christian doctors who had applied themselves to the study of letters and philosophy, soon abandoned the frequented paths, and *struck out into the devious wilds of fancy*. The Egyptians distinguished themselves in this new method of explaining the truth. They looked upon it as a noble and glorious task to bring the doctrines of celestial wisdom into a certain subjection to the precepts of their philosophy, and to make deep and profound researches into the intimate and hidden nature of those truths which the divine Saviour had delivered to his disciples. Origen was at the head of this speculative tribe. This great man, enchanted by the charms of the *Platonic philosophy*, set it up as the test of all religion, and imagined, that the reasons of each doctrine were *to be found in that favorite philosophy, and their nature and extent, to be determined by it*. It must be confessed that he handled this matter with modesty and with caution; but he still, gave an example to his disciples, the abuse of which could not fail to be pernicious, and under the authority of which, they would naturally indulge themselves without restraint in every wanton fancy. And so, indeed, the case was; for the disciples of Origen, breaking forth from the limits fixed by their master, *interpreted, in the most licentious manner*, the divine truths of *religion according to the tenor of Platonic philosophy.* From these teachers the *philosophical or scholastic theology* derives its origin."[78]

Mosheim says: "Origen unquestionably stands at the head of the interpreters of the Bible in this century. But with pain it must be added, he was first among those who have found in the Scriptures a secure retreat for all errors and idle fancies. *As this most ingenious man could see no possible method of vindicating all that is said in the Scriptures against the cavils of the heretics* and the enemies of Christianity, *provided he interpreted the language of the bible literally*, he concluded that he must expound the sacred volume *in the way in which the Platonists were accustomed to explain the history of their gods.*"[79]

Murdock, in his notes, says: "Origen perversely turned a large part of Biblical history into moral fables and many of the laws into allegories. Probably he learned this in the school of Ammonius, which expounded Hesiod, Homer, and the whole fabulous history of the Greeks allegorically. The predecessors of Origen, who searched after a mystical sense of Scripture, still set a high value on the *grammatical, or literal, sense;* but he often expresses himself, as if he attached no value to it. Before him allegories were resorted to, only to discover predictions of future events and rules for moral conduct; but he betook himself to allegories *in order to establish the principles of his philosophy* on a Scriptural basis....His propensity to allegories must be ascribed to the fertility of his invention, the *prevailing custom* of the Egyptians, *his education, the instructions he received from his teachers,* and the example both of the philosophers, of whom he was an admirer, and of the Jews....He hoped, by means of his allegories, more easily to convince the Jews, to confute the gnostics, and to silence the objections of both. But we must not forget his attachment to that system of philosophy which he embraced. *This philosophy could not be reconciled with the Scriptures ... and therefore the Scriptures must be interpreted allegorically*, that they might not contradict his philosophy....As the body is the baser part of man, so the literal is the less worthy sense of Scripture; and as the body often betrays good men into sin, so the literal sense often leads us into error."

Mosheim himself tells us how Origen determined when a passage should be interpreted literally and when allegorically: "Whenever the words, if understood literally, will afford a valuable meaning, one that is worthy of God, useful to men, and accordant with truth and correct reason, *then the literal meaning is to be retained;* but whenever the words, if understood literally, will express what is absurd, *or false, or contrary to correct reason, or useless, or unworthy of God,* then the literal sense is to be discarded, and the moral and mystical alone to be regarded. This rule he applies to every part both of the Old Testament and the New." This reasoning is sufficiently strong for any of our modern *higher critics.* If it led directly to the removal of the Word of God from the common people of the Middle Ages, because teachers adjudged no minds but their own capable of determining whether a certain passage should be interpreted literally or allegorically, to what will the same treatment of the Scriptures now lead? And if the disciples of Origen, lacking the caution of the great teacher, were led into the gross licentiousness of the heathen, how much of the wickedness of modern society should be attributed to the spirit of higher criticism, echoed from the pulpit, and breathed from the schoolroom?

Mosheim continues: "He [Origen] assigns two reasons why fables and literal absurdities are admitted into the Sacred Volume. The first is, that if the literal meaning were always rational and good, the reader would be apt to rest in it, and not look after the moral and mystical sense. The second is, that fabulous and incongruous representations often afford moral and mystical instructions which could not so well be conveyed by sober facts and representations."

Perhaps this is enough to show that scholasticism, or a philosophical interpretation of the Scriptures had its origin in the Christian schools. By this it is plain why these youth became papists, instead of followers of the meek and lowly Galilean. There was no other theory which could, so effectually as this, have stamped out faith. No other teaching than this same higher criticism could have more truly, developed that power which "speaketh great words against the Most High, and thinketh to change times and laws." It formed the beast in the third century; it is forming the image to the beast in the present century. Students under such instruction had received ample preparation for a belief in the right of the church to interpret Scripture, and a belief in the infallibility of the pope.

We have seen the origin of two of the streams which, uniting, helped swell the torrent of the papacy. There are still other tributaries to this mighty river. Each rises somewhere in heathendom, flows with a devious course, but finally, as if in accordance with some great natural law, unites with those other currents in forming the mystery of iniquity. Each stream is an educational principle, opposed in itself to Christianity; but instead of being lost in the depths of the main channel, it seems to develop greater power of doing evil, and brings its adherents into more complete degradation after the mingling than before.

The third principle which presents itself for analysis is known as *mysticism*. Both the teachings of Clement and the scholasticism of Origen exalted reason above faith. Mysticism was advocated by Origen and later by Augustine. It is defined as "that faculty of reason, from which proceeds the health and vigor of the mind,... an emanation from God into the human soul, and comprehended in it the principles and elements of all truth, human and divine."[80] There is a spark of divinity in every man. It is the object of Christian education to develop the image of Christ in the human being; but with the mystics, it was maintained that "silence, tranquility, repose, and solitude, accompanied with such acts of mortification as might tend to extenuate and exhaust the body, were the means by which the hidden and internal word was excited to produce its latent virtues and to instruct men in the knowledge of divine things."

It is not so much with the doctrine as with the results which were wrought by the teachings of such doctrine, that we are concerned. From an adherence to this method of reasoning arose the whole monkish system; for, says Mosheim, "This method of reasoning produced strange effects, and drove many into caves and deserts, where they macerated their bodies with hunger and thirst, and submitted to all the miseries of the severest discipline that a gloomy imagination could prescribe." Egypt soon swarmed with these fanatics, and the whole history of the Dark Ages circles around them. They broke the bonds of family affection, overturned governments, and seated popes. Draper, speaking of the monks, says: "It is said that there were at one time in that country [Egypt] of these religious recluses not fewer than seventy-six thousand males and twenty-seven thousand females. With countless other uncouth forms, under the hot sun of that climate they seemed to be spawned from the mud of the Nile." "From Egypt and Syria monachism spread like an epidemic." "It was significantly observed that the road to ecclesiastical elevation lay through the monastery porch, and often *ambition contentedly wore for a season the cowl, that it might seize more surely the miter.*"[81]

We shall need to study the monastic system as the repositories of learning in the Dark Ages, and therefore give but a passing glance at the origin of the order in the doctrine of mysticism. Its evils cannot be portrayed without a blush, and it was against this system, taking as it did into its clutches the education of the masses, that the Reformation thrust its weight. We have seen truth *struggling* against error. It was in the *schools of the early Christians* that wisdom *by faith* was taught. It was *into these same schools* that pagan philosophy crept. It was the teacher who espoused this philosophy, and again a teacher who opposed it. Students imbibed the ideas of the leading educators, and became church teachers. The strongest minds, turning from the Word, and that alone, became expounders of philosophy and the sciences.

Gradually error prevailed, until in the schools, almost entirely in monastic hands, truth was so covered that D'Aubigné's description of the work of the schoolmen of the Dark Ages is striking. He says: "These industrious artisans of thought had unraveled every theological idea, and of all their threads had woven a web, under which it would have been difficult for more skillful persons than their contemporaries to recognize the truth in its pristine purity."

It is not the province of this chapter to deal with theological controversies in themselves. It is only as these controversies took possession of and molded the courses of study in the schools; only as they found their strongest supporters in the persons of teachers, and were carried to the world by students, that our attention is drawn to another line of argument, which, as it were, clenched the work of the papacy, and gave it its power over the minds of men.

Quoting again from D'Aubigné: "The *Pelagian* doctrine, expelled by Augustine from the church when it had presented itself boldly, insinuated itself as demi-Pelagianism, and under the mask of the Augustine forms of expression. This error spread with astonishing rapidity throughout Christendom. The danger of the doctrine was particularly manifested in this—that by placing goodness without, and not within, the heart, it set a great value on external actions, legal observances, and penitential works.... Whilst Pelagianism corrupted the Christian doctrine, it *strengthened the hierarchy*....When it laid down a doctrine that man could attain a state of perfect sanctification, it affirmed also that the merits of saints and martyrs might be applied to the church. Pelagianism multiplied rites and ceremonies.

"But it was especially by the *system of penance*, which flowed immediately from Pelagianism, that Christianity was perverted. At first, *penance* had consisted in certain public expressions of repentance....By degrees it was extended to every sin, even to the most secret....Instead of looking to Christ for pardon, through faith alone, it was sought for principally in the church through penitential works....*Flagellations* were superadded to these practices....They accordingly invented that system of barter celebrated under the title of *Indulgences*....A bull of Clement VII declared it an article of faith....The philosophers of Alexandria had spoken of a fire in which men were to be purified. *Many ancient doctors* had adopted this notion; and Rome declared this philosophical opinion a tenet of the church. *The pope by a bull annexed purgatory to his domain.*"[82] "The Catholic Church was not the papacy," says D'Aubigné "The latter was the oppressor, the former the oppressed." Draper tersely defines the papacy as "the tyranny of theology over thought."

Men departed from the simplicity of a summary gospel by faith. Reason and scientific research took the place of faith in the Word. Education turned men's minds from God to self, and reason was exalted. The papacy was thus formed. If we look for a visible union of the church and the state before recognizing it as the papacy, we shall find ourselves entrapped; *for it is the working out of a system of education based on human philosophy that forms the papacy;* and the holy which adopts this system of education naturally turns to the state for support.

It is because of the truth of this statement that the papacy wields its influence through its schools; this is why it has always feared a revival of learning more than the combined forces of all the armies of the world. A death-blow to the papacy can be struck only by introducing a system of education founded upon the teachings of Christ, placing God's Word as guide, and inspiring faith as the one avenue to wisdom.

Chapter XI
Education of the Middle Ages

THE development of the papacy led directly to the Dark Ages, for "the noontide of the papacy was the world's moral midnight." The papacy was the logical working out of an educational scheme; hence the moral darkness which spread over the world during the prophetic period of twelve hundred and sixty years was due to wrong methods of education. People do not sink into degradation and sin when properly educated. Truth elevates, and, when embodied in man, brings him nearer to his Maker. Faith is the ladder by which he climbs, and when that element has been lacking in an educational system, the masses have sunk lower and lower.

The mind is a wonderful thing, the most profound study of the universe. It was designed to be free, to grasp the mighty laws of its own Creator, and a means was supplied by which that very thing could be done: "If any of you lack wisdom, let him ask of God...But let him ask in faith, nothing wavering."

In order to maintain the supremacy thus gained, it was necessary for the education of the young to lie wholly within the control of the papal hierarchy; and it is with their educational institutions and educational methods that we have now to deal. It is hoped that the study of the Dark Ages will so accentuate the importance of Protestants' maintaining their own schools, that the tendency now so strong in the other direction may receive a check. The education begun in the schools of the early Christians has been followed into the monastic institutions of the Middle Ages. The life and power of Christianity departed, and form alone remained. It has been said that "paganism in the garb of Christianity walked into the church," and it can truthfully be added that *it gained admittance through the schools.*

In order to trace carefully the education offered by the papacy—and that comprised all that was then offered—the first quotations are concerning primary instruction. Laurie says: "Instruction began about the age of seven. The *alphabet*, written on tables or leaves, was learned by heart by the children, then *syllables and words*. The first reading-book was the Latin Psalter, and this was read again and again *until it could be said by heart;* and numerous priests, and even monks, were content all their lives with the mere sound of Latin words, which they could both read and recite, but did not understand."[83]

Note carefully that work for these children was almost wholly *memory* work. They were to *learn by heart* and to *repeat without understanding*. This was the first step in that great system which binds the minds of the masses to the will of one sovereign mind.

"Writing followed." "The elements of arithmetic were also taught, but merely with a view to the calculation of church days and festivals."[84] "Latin was begun very early (apparently immediately after the psaltery was known), with the *learning by heart* of declensions and conjugations and lists of vocables. The rule was to use Latin in the school in conversing....In the eleventh century, if not earlier, Latin conversation-books… were not only read, but, like everything else, *learned by heart*."[85] Their method of studying Latin emphasizes the thought of the formal abstract way of teaching, which tended to conservatism and mental subjection. "Memory is the faculty that subordinates the present under the past, and its extensive training develops a habit of mind that holds by what is prescribed, and recoils from the new and untried. In short, the educational curriculum that lays great stress on memorizing, produces a class of conservative people."[86] The papal schools employed methods which, in themselves, in the course of a few generations would develop dependent rather than independent thinking; therefore, methods are as important as the subject taught. Again, it is well to remember that there was a deep design in making the Latin tongue universal. It was one of the ways by which the papacy kept its control of all nations and tongues. Draper explains it thus:—

"The unity of the church, and, therefore, *its power*, required the use of Latin as a sacred language. Through this Rome had stood in an attitude strictly European, and was enabled to maintain a general international relation. It gave her far more power than her asserted celestial authority.... Their officials could pass without difficulty into every nation, and communicate without embarrassment with each other, from Ireland to Bohemia, from Italy to Scotland."[87]

The character of the youth was formed, says Painter, from memorizing "the *fables of Aesop* and collections of maxims and proverbs. After this, Virgil was usually the text-book, and was handled in the same style."

Of the monastic schools Mosheim says: "In most of the schools, the so-called seven liberal arts were taught. The pupil commenced with grammar, then proceeded to rhetoric, and afterward to logic or dialectics. Having thus mastered the Trivium, as it was called, those who aspired to greater attainments proceeded with slow steps through the *Quadrivium* [a course including arithmetic, music, geometry, and astronomy] to the honor of perfectly learned men."[88]

Says Painter: "Seven years were devoted to the completion of the course in liberal arts [the Trivium and the Quadrivium]....Dialectic or logic was based somewhat remotely on the writings of Aristotle. At a later period, logic was rigidly applied to the development of theology, and gave rise to a class of scholars called the schoolmen....Arithmetic was imperfectly taught, importance being attached to the supposed secret properties of numbers.

Geometry was taught in an abridged form, while astronomy did not differ materially from astrology. The study of music consisted chiefly in learning to chant the hymns of the church."[89]

Mosheim thus continues his description of the work of the schools in the eleventh century. "This course of study, adopted in all the schools of the West, was not a little changed after the middle of this century. For logic,... having been improved by the reflection and skill of certain close thinkers, and being taught more fully and acutely, acquired such an ascendancy in the minds of the majority, that they neglected grammar, rhetoric, and the other sciences, both the elegant and the abstruse, and devoted their whole lives to dialectics, or to logical and metaphysical discussions. For whoever was well acquainted with dialectics, or what we call logic and metaphysics, was supposed to possess learning enough, and to lose nothing by being ignorant of all other branches of learning....In this age, the philosophy of the Latins was confined wholly to what they called dialectics; and the other branches of philosophy were unknown even by name. Moreover, their dialectics was miserably dry and barren."[90]

This is sufficient, perhaps, on the use of language and logic, and we turn to geography and some of the sciences. Even the children today will smile at the teachings of some of the church fathers on the subject of geography. Says Draper: "In the Patristic Geography the earth is a flat surface bordered by the waters of the sea, on the yielding support of which rests the crystalline dome of the sky. These doctrines were for the most part supported by passages from the Holy Scriptures, perversely wrested from their proper meaning. Thus Cosmas Indicopleustes, whose Patristic Geography had been an authority for nearly eight hundred years, triumphantly disposed of the sphericity of the earth by demanding of its advocates, how, in the day of judgment, men on the other side of a globe could see the Lord descending through the air!"[91]

It was in opposition to such theories, and a hundred absurdities concerning the ocean, the boiling waters of the equator, the serpents in the West, etc., that Columbus, De Gama, and other explorers had to contend; and one of the most wonderful effects of the work of these navigators was the thrust given papal education. A wound was then received which was incurable.

If, in the mind of the reader, the question arises, Why should the papal schools teach such things? Simply consider that the whole system of papal theology was intended to make the people feel that the world was the center of the universe, and that the pope was the center of the world. Christ and his position in creation were usurped by the head of the church. This was the papacy.

This could be brought about *only by education*, and could be maintained only as generation after generation was *taught* from infancy to old age to place faith in man, not God. Not only the subjects taught, but the manner of teaching them, served well the purpose of the papacy. Only within the last few years, comparatively speaking, have our own schools seen the necessity of breaking away from some of those relics of the educational system of the Dark Ages.

Memory work, pure and simple, has given way in a great measure to research and experiment, even in the primary grades. The alphabet is no longer driven into the childish mind by the ferule, nor kept there by mere force of repetition. The advanced methods in dealing with the mind are a step in the right direction. The pity is that educators, while groping for light, while casting off some of the moth-eaten garments of past ages, have failed to see the cause of the evil, and deal so largely with results instead of removing the cause. The evil began by renouncing the Scriptures and faith in Holy Writ as a part of education. The spirit and power will accompany reform only when these are replaced in their proper setting. While educators of the world are realizing the need of a change in methods, it is time for them to see also the need of a change in subject matter and text-books. *Protestants* in particular *should arouse* to the times. If the study of paganism, instead of Christianity or truth, produced the Dark Ages, and if wrong methods held the minds of men and prolonged that darkness, forbidding the shining of the light, it is time for both *methods and material* to be reconstructed in the schools of today.

We can with profit notice the attitude of the papal schools toward some of the sciences, taking for example that most practical of modern branches, the science of medicine. What was the work of the physician during the Dark Ages? Draper says: "Physicians were viewed by the church with dislike, and regarded as atheists by the people, who held firmly to the lessons they had been taught, that cures must be wrought by relics of martyrs and bones of saints, by prayers and intercessions."[92]

It is well to remember that Christ was the Great Physician, healing not only soul maladies, but physical infirmities as well; and to the apostles was given the commission to heal the sick and restore sight to the blind. Gradually, however, as the power of the gospel in its purity was lost by the substitution of error for truth, the leaders of the church introduced miracle cures, and preached the efficacy of the bones of saints, etc., in the cure of disease. This became popular, and increased throughout the Dark Ages.

Draper describes the fanaticism of the monastic schools, and finally assigns a reason for the exclusion from them of the study of physiology and anatomy and the science of medicine. "The body," he says, "was under some spiritual charge—the first joint of the right thumb being in the care of God the Father, the second under that of the blessed Virgin, and so on of other parts. For each disease there was a saint. A man with sore eyes must invoke St. Clara, but if it were an inflammation elsewhere, he must turn to St. Anthony....For the propitiation of these celestial beings it was necessary that fees should be paid, and thus the practice of imposture—medicine became a great source of profit. In all this there was no other intention than that of extracting money."[93]

While such was the teachings of the papacy, the Jews and Mohammedans were achieving wonderful success, and making discoveries of lasting benefit to mankind in Spain and Asia Minor. "Bishops, princes, kings, and popes had each in private his Hebrew doctor; though all understood, that he was a contraband luxury, in many countries pointedly and absolutely prohibited by the law. In the eleventh century nearly all the physicians in Europe were Jews." One reason for this was: "The church would tolerate no interference with her spiritual methods of treating disease, which formed one of her most productive sources of gain; and the study of medicine had been formally introduced into the rabbinical schools."[94]

The bitter hatred of the papacy toward independence of mind is well illustrated in the treatment that the Jewish physicians received from the popes. Draper says: "The school at Salerno was still sending forth its doctors. In Rome, Jewish physicians were numerous, the popes themselves employing them....At this period Spain and France were full of learned Jews; and perhaps partly by their exerting too much influence upon the higher classes with whom they came in contact (for the physician of a Christian prince was very often the rival of his confessor), and partly because the practice of medicine, as they pursued it, interfered with the gains of the church, the clergy took alarm, and caused to be re-enacted or enforced the ancient laws. The Council of Beziers (A. D. 1246) and the Council of Alby (A. D. 1254) prohibited all Christians from resorting to the services of an Israelitish physician."[95]

To show that this was a matter which concerned the *schools*, and in proof of the statement that papal schools still adhere to formalism, miracle cure, and relic worship, we need only to notice that "the faculty of Paris [University], awakening at last to the danger of the case, caused, A. D. 130I, a decree to be published prohibiting either man or woman of the religion of Moses from practicing medicine upon any person of the Catholic religion. A similar course was pursued in Spain. At this time the Jews were confessedly at the head of French medicine. It was the appointment of one of their persuasion, Profatius, *as regent* of the faculty of Montpellier, A. D. 1300, which drew upon them the wrath of the faculty of Paris."

"The animosity of the French ecclesiastics against the Jewish physicians at last led to the banishment of all the Jews from France, A. D. 1306."[96] The papal universities were unwilling to teach medicine, and finding that the Jewish schools of science were greatly weakening papal authority in France, this race was banished bodily.

Comparing this history with the present work of the medical fraternity, and especially with that class of medical students whose life work is to spread the gospel while relieving the body, one better understands that physiology should be the basis of every educational effort, and the place that it and kindred sciences should occupy in the courses of instruction, pursued by our children, youth, and maturer minds; and also the cause of that spiritual darkness which is even now hanging over the world, and for centuries held Europe in its clutches; but it shall be pierced by Christian education.

The papacy, in case of opposition which threatened her authority, had two methods of procedure. The first was an attempt to annihilate both the trouble and the troublers. Thus, she simply banished all Jews from France that her own universities might not be overshadowed by the light of truth. Her second method of procedure was a counter-reformation; that is, if a reform in education arose outside the church which threatened to undermine her doctrines, it might be met by a partial reform within her borders, the reform going only so far as was absolutely necessary to satisfy the cravings of minds that dared think for themselves. It was not always possible to completely crush a reformation, or the reformers; and as was quite often the case in the schools, studies which could not be entirely banished, were taught, but in such a way as best to conserve the needs of the church. That medicine, as well as law, was taught in the higher papal schools, cannot be denied. Says Mosheim: "The seven liberal arts [The Trivium and the Quadrivium] were gradually included under the term *philosophy*, to which were added *theology, jurisprudence,* and *medicine.* And thus, these four *faculties*, as they are called, were in the next century formed in the universities."[97] But in the study of medicine, as in philosophy or law, memory work devoid of understanding—the form without the spirit—was the characteristic. As the saints and martyrs in theology had taken the place of the Greek gods and goddesses, so in the study of other branches a multitude of pagan terms, clothed with what was then known as the "Christian spirit," was made to satisfy the longing for real mental culture. The simplicity of the gospel was laid aside. What God had revealed was made to appear too complex for the human mind, and the secret things which are known only to God were pried into. In theology, dialectics, or logic, became the study of endless queries, difficult syllogisms, meaningless quibbles. Men delighted in propounding such questions as, "How many angels can stand on the point of a needle?" and others prided themselves on the acuteness of their reasoning powers in arguing such questions. Likewise, in medicine, the study of the simple needs of the body and the rational treatment of disease was obscured by hundreds of *Latin terms*, and these were memorized to the neglect of the simple philosophy of the science. It is with this multitude of names, hoary with age, and savoring strongly of their pagan origin, that the student of medicine is still compelled to grapple.

The history of the rise of European universities throws light on the attitude of the papacy toward education. While Europe was overspread by spiritual and intellectual darkness, God used another people to disseminate truth.

When faith in God was lost, and in its place was substituted that blind faith in man and obedience to the church which is known in European history as the age of faith, learning was propagated by the Arabs. That power which had failed to conquer the world by the sword, now gained by intellectual culture what the arms of Mohammed and his immediate successors failed to achieve. Spain, while in the hands of the Moors, contributed more to European civilization than at any other time in her history; and it was as an *educator* and through the *influence of her schools* that the papacy received its blow from the south which made her more readily succumb to the revolt of Germany under Luther. By the Arabs "flourishing schools were established in all the principal cities, notably at Bagdad and Damascus in the East, and at Cordova, Salamanca, and Toledo in the West. Here grammar, mathematics, astronomy, philosophy, chemistry, and medicine were pursued with great ardor and success. The Arabians originated chemistry, discovering alcohol, and nitric and sulphuric acids. They gave algebra and trigonometry their modern form; applied the pendulum to the reckoning of time; ascertained the size of the earth by measuring a degree, and made catalogues of the stars."[98] And all this was done when Europe as a whole was lying in darkness, when the chemist was considered a wizard, when astronomy was merely astrology, and whatever learning existed was formal and spiritless.

But the discoveries of the Arab teachers could not long remain with them alone, and it is with the spread of their ideas through the schools by means of the students that we are concerned. "For a time, they [the Arabs] were the intellectual leaders of Europe. Their schools in Spain were largely attended by Christian youth from other European countries, who carried back with them to their homes the Arabian science, and through it stimulated intellectual activity in Christian [papal] nations."[99]

The specialization of studies such as theology, medicine, or philosophy, together with the impulse derived from the Mohammedans in Africa and the Arabs in Spain, led to the establishment of the universities, which were, as before stated, composed of four faculties, or colleges. "They arose independently of both church and state." The University of

Paris "became the most distinguished seat of learning in Europe. At one time it was attended by more than twenty thousand students."

The growth of the universities was very rapid, and they threatened speedily to revolutionize the society of Europe and overthrow the papal hierarchy. "The influence and power of the universities were speedily recognized," says Painter; "and though originally free associations, they were soon brought into relation with the church and the state, by which they were officially authorized and endowed." If learning could not be suppressed, then it must be controlled by the church; and the "church sought to attach them [the universities] to itself, in order to join to the power of faith the power of knowledge. The first privileges that the universities received proceeded from the popes." "While Rome was not the mother, she was yet the nurse of universities." Scientific investigation had by this time received such an impulse from youth who had been students in the Arab schools that the church could not hope to crush it. The only hope of the papacy was to so surround the truth with fables and mysteries, and to so conduct the schools, that again the spirit of progress would be lost in its labyrinthine wanderings through empty forms. *Monopoly in education* works havoc in the same way that a monopoly in commerce leads to oppression. And so it was.

"The students led a free and uncontrolled life, seeking and finding protection in their own university authorities even from the civil power."[100]

Youth from the age of twelve and upward attended these universities, making it necessary to teach the secondary studies which terminated in a bachelor's degree. "Boys... attended the Parisian university merely for instruction in... grammar, rhetoric, and dialectic; and after three or four years' study they received the title of Baccalaureus." "When he reached... the age of seventeen or eighteen, he then began the study for the mastership."[101]

It will be remembered that the schools established by the early church were marked for the simplicity of their methods, and their singleness of purpose. Their object was to educate workers for the spread of the gospel. For the accomplishment of this object the course of instruction was arranged, and students were sent forth into the world commissioned of God, as were the disciples after their ordination. There was no call for the granting of degrees. These, it is true, were used in the pagan schools, and indicated that the receiver had been initiated, after years of study, into the hidden mysteries of Greek wisdom. Among the pagans, indeed, the principle of degrees and diplomas dated back to the days of Egyptian and Babylonian supremacy, where it was indicative of fellowship in the grossest forms of licentiousness.

Greece, the country which united the learning of Babylon and the wisdom of Egypt, and offered it to Europe in the form of Platonism, naturally enough made use of diplomas and degrees. And the fact that her wisdom was so complicated in its nature made it necessary to spend long years in mastering her sciences.

Paganism, moreover, has but one model for all men; its aim is ever to crush individuality and mold all characters alike. To accomplish this purpose the schools arranged their studies in courses, demanding that each student should pass over the same ground. This is characteristic of all educational systems aside from that one, the true education, which comes from God. If you look to China, you find it there, as it develops the disciples of Confucius; India educates her Brahmans in the same manner; the priests and wise men of Egypt were taught in schools of a similar type. The Jews had aped the fashion of the pagan world, and it was from this custom that Christ called his disciples. One of the surest signs that the schools established in the days of Christian purity had lost the spirit which characterized the apostolic teaching, is the fact that the schools of the Middle Ages had adopted this pagan custom.

Students were called into the universities when mere boys, and by hundreds and thousands were run through the "grind" which we term "course of instruction," and were turned out at the end of ten, twenty, and sometimes even forty years with a degree, which, in dignity, corresponded to the years spent in completing the course.

This custom is papal. It is opposed to the very spirit of Christianity; and any institution of learning which deigns to accept the approval of the state, while at the same time passing as a Christian institution, is not only linking itself with the papacy, but with paganism as well. Of His followers Christ says, "They are not of the world, even as I am not of the world."

"Older students, those especially in the theological faculty, with their fifteen or sixteen years' course of study, achieved in this respect far greater notoriety. At the age of thirty or forty the student at the university was still a scholar."[102] The idea of long courses is not, then, a modern one, and American colleges can truthfully point to the university of Paris for the precedent in this respect as in some others. In the granting of degrees another interesting subject is approached. Laurie continues: "Up to the middle of the twelfth century, anyone taught in the infant universities who thought he had the requisite knowledge....In the second half of the twelfth century, when bishops and abbots, who acted, personally or through their deputies, as chancellors of the rising university schools, wished to assume to themselves exclusively the right of granting the license,... Pope Alexander III forbade them, on the ground that the teaching faculty was a gift of God."[103] This, however, must have been the work of a liberal pope, for earlier—that is, in 1219—"Pope Honorius III interfered with the granting of degrees; and in order to impose a check on abuses, directed that they should be conferred not by, but by permission of, the archdeacon of the cathedral, and under his presidency."[104]

The church had gained control of the universities, and through her representative, usually the chancellor, *granted degrees*. Now, in order to keep the authority well in her own hands, no one was allowed to teach who did not hold a license granted by the university after an examination. Thus, the educational *trust* developed, and the iron hand of Rome, though concealed in a silken glove, clinched her victories, and strove to crush all opponents.

Our modern B.S., M.A., LL.D., D.D. etc. were adopted into the universities at this stage of educational history. "Itter informs us," says Laurie, "that…a complete university course was represented by *four degrees—bachelor, master, licentiate,* and finally *doctor,* which last was usually taken at the age of thirty or thirty-five." "The next development of the degree system was the introduction of the *grades of bachelor* and *master,* or licentiate, into each of the higher faculties—theology, law, and medicine. Thus, a man who had finished his preliminary art studies, generally at the age of twenty-one, and wished to specialize in theology, medicine, or law, had to pass through the stages of *bachelor of theology,* or of medicine, or of law, and then of *master* or licentiate, before he obtained the title of *doctor.* The *bachelorship* of medicine or law was reached in three years, of theology in seven. Four years' further study brought the *doctor's degree.*"[105] "The conferring of degrees was originated by a pope."[106] The educational monopoly appeared quite complete; and having gained the form of godliness and the civil power, the old scheme of killing the life and substituting those things which would recognize the papal hierarchy, were again introduced. Leading educators are awakening to the true situation. Christian education alone can deliver.

"The moral tone of the universities was low," says Painter; "there were brawls, outbreaks, and abominable immoralities. 'The students,' say the Vienna statutes, 'shall not spend more time in drinking, fighting, and guitar playing than at physics, logic, and the regular courses of lectures; and they shall not get up public dances in the streets. Quarrelers, wanton persons, drunkards, those that go about serenading at night, or who spend their leisure in following after lewd women; thieves, those that insult citizens, players at dice—having been properly warned and not reforming, besides the ordinary punishment provided by law for those misdemeanors, shall be deprived of their academical privileges and expelled.' These prohibitions give us a clear insight into university life of the time, for it was not worse at Vienna than at Paris and elsewhere."[107]

Could some of those medieval students be resurrected and placed in some of the universities of the nineteenth century, they might feel quite at home, not only as far as courses of study and the granting of degrees is concerned, but in revelings, parties, etc., judging from the reports of the hazing, drinking, and general carousing of the students in our university towns."[108]

The conduct of students is the reflex of the instruction given. It is not, therefore, to be wondered at that the instruction of the universities, containing as it did the form without the life, should fail to develop stability of character in its students.

"The true Catholic attitude to all investigation was, and is, one admitting of great advances in every department of learning, while checking all true freedom of thought."[109]

The *North American Review* for October, 1842, expresses in concise language the relation of students and schools to the general government and consequent state of society. It says: "In the colleges is determined the character of most of the persons who are to fill the professions, teach the schools, write the books, and do most of the business of legislation for the whole body of the people. The general direction of literature and politics, the prevailing habits and modes of thought throughout the country, are in the hands of men whose social position and early advantages have given them an influence, of the magnitude and permanency of which the possessors themselves are hardly conscious."

Recognizing this fact, the papacy controlled the education of the Middle Ages, and is today seeking to do the same thing. Luther and other reformers, also recognizing this fact, sought to overthrow the tyranny of the papacy by establishing new schools where freedom of thought would be fostered through faith in God's Word.

Protestants today, looking upon the system of education as it now exists, and tracing there the same long courses in the classics and the sciences; the same degrees granted in a manner similar to the Dark Ages, the text-book containing the same theories, the same terms, the same doctrines of philosophy; the same tendency toward monarchism, or the monopoly of education by certain universities, and through them by the same power that has borne sway, should, for the sake of their government, and for the sake of their faith, establish schools of their own. As the papacy, by the subjection of thought, builds up a monarchy in place of democracy; as she in the same way overthrows faith in God, substituting faith in man or the church, so *Protestant schools should educate children* in the pure principles of that gospel freedom which recognizes the equality of every man in the sight of heaven, and makes it possible for the government to be of, for, and by the people by developing the Christian character through faith in Jesus Christ.

Chapter XII
The Sixteenth Century
Reformation
An Educational Reform

WHILE following the history of education through the
Dark Ages, we have often been compelled to recognize that an influence was at work slowly but surely undermining the structure which the papacy was, with the greatest perseverance, erecting, and which that power purposed should withstand all the attacks brought against it. The papacy had calculated well; it had, in absorbing the educational system of the times, laid its hand on the very tap-root of society, and, in its education as well as in its doctrines, woven about the human race meshes which only the Prince of heaven could rend with the sword of eternal truth.

Never has the world seen such an enduring system as the papacy. Patterned so nearly after the truth of God, and resembling so closely, both in church government and educational principles, the plan delivered to the chosen nation, that only an expert, guided by the Spirit of truth, could judge between the true and the counterfeit, it had, as had the Jews before them, replaced the life by the mere form. Nevertheless, so firmly laid was the foundation, and so substantially built were the walls, that for centuries it baffled all attempts at overthrow.

This structure had as its foundation an *educational system*; the mortar which held the bricks in the wall was *educational methods*, and should the building fall, the foundation itself must be attacked.

As a civil power, the papacy was periodically attacked by ambitious kings and princes; but these shocks scarcely disturbed the serenity of the papal head, so firm was his throne. The sword of the Mohammedans was broken at Tours; and the Crescent, instead of advancing to the full by encircling the Mediterranean, waned as its light receded to the shores of Africa and the west of Asia.

What the Turk could not do by force of arms, he did in another way. In 1453 Constantinople fell into the hands of the calif, yet this did not affect the strength of the papal hierarchy. But as the Turk came into Greece, Greek art and literature fled to Italy. Here is the attack on the papacy which came from the east. Painter says: "The revival of classical learning, which had its central point in the downfall of Constantinople in 1453, exerted a favorable influence. It opened the literary treasures of Greece and Rome, provided a new culture for the mind, awakened dissatisfaction with the scholastic teaching of the church, and tended to emancipate thought from subjection to ecclesiastical authority."[110] The taking of Constantinople did still more toward hastening the Reformation. Venice had controlled the commerce of the eastern Mediterranean, but Turkish supremacy in those waters transferred that power to her rival, Genoa, on the other side of Italy; and from this latter center began the search for a western passage to the East Indies which led to the accidental discovery of America.

Again, "The revival of learning was so intimately related to the Reformation, and to the educational advancement dating from that time, that it calls for consideration in some detail. It had its origin in Italy....Eager scholars from England, France, and Germany sat at the feet of Italian masters, in order afterward to bear beyond the Alps the precious seed of the new culture."[111] However, this Greek culture, or new learning, was nothing more nor less than a revival of the study of Greek paganism. Notwithstanding that fact, a life and enthusiasm attended its study which drew students from the papal universities, and induced men to travel hundreds of miles for the sake of sitting at the feet of masters of the Greek classics.

This was the attempted reform of the papacy made by classic literature. Its results cannot but interest us. Painter further says: "The revival of letters produced different re-sults in different countries. Everywhere it contributed to the emancipation of the human mind, but in Italy it tended strongly to paganize its adherents."

Bear in mind that the classics were attempting to reform the papacy. Here was the result in Italy. Italian schools un-doubtedly needed reforming, for the words of Luther describ-ing German schools are applicable to all papal institutions. Of these he said: "What have they been taught in the universities and convents, but to become blockheads? A man has studied *twenty, forty* years, and has learned neither Latin nor German. But as much as reform was needed, Greek classics "in Italy tended strongly to paganize its adherents." We cannot look for the classics, then, to Christianize the Italian papists.

But while "in Italy the new learning became a minis-ter of infidelity, in Germany [it became a minister] of re-ligion." Why this difference? The work of Erasmus, Lu-ther, and Melanchthon, as they introduced the study of the Greek and Hebrew Scriptures into the German schools, will answer why. The Italians studied the Greek classics for the *thought*, and it paganized its adherents; the Germans studied the Greek New Testament, translating it into the mother tongue, and it became one of the greatest helps in the spread of the Reformation of the sixteenth century.

So much for the attempted reform by Greek classics. They played their part, but they could not overthrow the papacy; and why should we expect it when papal education was, in the first place, built upon those same classics and the philosophy of Greek writers?

We now turn to the southern attack upon the papal system. This was also an educational attack. Already we have seen the Arab schools in Spain. Before the eleventh century Christian youth attended these schools, taking across the Pyrenees the science of the Moors. The papacy quailed before this attack, and in order to lessen its force, the sciences of the Arabs were adopted in the papal universities. This, as we have already seen, was done in medicine and mathematics. But again, the form was retained without the life. France, because of her jealousy of the Jewish physicians, through the influence of the University of Paris, banished every Jew from her borders. *A scientific attack could not overthrow the papacy.* However, the Moors went quietly on in their scientific discoveries; and when the fall of Constantinople closed the eastern route to the Indian Ocean, and Genoa wanted a western route, Spain was prepared to offer sailors the necessary charts and maps, compasses, and other mariners' instruments. Her astronomical studies, celestial maps, and measurements of the degrees on the earth's surface encouraged voyages both to the south and west, in direct contradiction to the theories of the patristic geographies.

When Columbus asked aid at the Spanish court to fit vessels for the tour across the Atlantic, it is strange to note that the wife of the king of Spain, who took from the Moors the keys of Granada, and drove the Arab and his learning out of Europe, was the same woman who pledged her jewels to this man—a man, who, dependent upon Arabic scientific investigation, discovered a world where those same truths might be planted, and mature untrammeled by papal tyranny. I say this was more than a coincidence. The hand of God was in it; and, as D'Aubigné says: "He prepares slowly and from afar that which he designs to accomplish. He has ages in which to work."

While scientific knowledge could not overthrow the papacy, it had its part to play along with the classics. When men were spiritually dead, and the Word of God was hidden, minds were freed from papal thralldom by the work of the scientist and the classical student. Bear in mind, however, that the classics helped only as they offered the Scriptures; and science helped only as it opened men's minds to the reception of the truths of God's Word. Mighty forces were at work: the earth itself must be moved, and the fulcrum whereon rested the lever by which it was to be turned in its orbit was the throne of God, and the *Word of the Eternal was the moving power.* Men, weak in themselves but resolute in purpose, were the instruments in the hand of God to accomplish a task which ages had waited for, and principalities and powers in heavenly places had longed to see.

The Reformation was not the work of a year, nor yet of one man, even in Germany it was the gradual work of a system of education, and that system was the same as had formerly been given to Israel, as had been exemplified and amplified in the life of Christ, and was at the time of the Reformation to be revealed, little by little, as men's minds, long darkened by oppression, were able to grasp it.

Agricola, known as the father of German humanism, was one of the earliest reformers, and his attitude as a teacher and his expressions concerning education prove the fact that the Reformation began in the educational institutions. This man was for a time "a pupil of Thomas à Kempis; he passed several years at the university of Louvain; subsequently he studied at Paris, and afterward in Italy," so that he was well acquainted with the institutions of the day. He became a teacher at Heidelberg. At the age of forty-one he began the study of Hebrew, in order to read the Hebrew Bible.

He was urged to take charge of a school at Antwerp, but refused, expressing his opinion of the school in this advice sent to the authorities: "It is necessary to exercise the greatest care in choosing a director for your school. Take neither a theologian nor a so-called rhetorician, who thinks he is able to speak of everything without understanding anything of eloquence. Such people make in school the same figure, according to the Greek proverb, that a dog does in a bath. It is necessary to seek a man resembling the phoenix of Achilles; that is, who knows how to teach, to speak, and to act at the same time. If you know such a man, get him at any price; for the matter involves the future of your children, whose tender youth receives with the same susceptibility the impress of good and of bad examples."

His ideas concerning methods were as clear as those expressed on the subject of schools and the character of the teacher. He was evidently able to see things in advance of his age, and in the spirit of a seer can truthfully be classed with the forerunners of the Reformation. In another letter he writes:

"Whoever wishes to study with success must exercise himself in these three things: in getting clear views of a subject; in fixing in his memory what he has understood; and in producing something from his own resources." Each of the three things specified cuts directly across the methods employed in papal schools, and which were so necessary to the stability of that hierarchy. This was the beginning of the Reformation as seen in education.

One more quotation from Agricola's letter emphasizes the thought that schools were then conducted where dry form and abstract memory work were giving place to thought—original thought. "It is necessary," he says, "to exercise one's self in composition; when we have produced nothing, what we have learned remains dead. The knowledge that we acquire ought to be like seed sown in the earth, germinating and bearing fruit."[112]

Reuchlin, one of Melanchthon's teachers, recognized the best means of winning opponents to the truth, and said: "The best way to convert the Israelites would be to establish two professors of the Hebrew language in each university, who should teach the theologians to read the Bible in Hebrew, and thus refute the Jewish doctors." The fact that such a position exposed Reuchlin to violent opposition from the monks and papal teachers shows that he rightly divined the remedy for papal oppression; and it is significant of an approaching reformation when he thus recommends that the Bible be placed in the universities for study by theologians.

There is a rift in the clouds, and ere long the sun will appear. But "men loved darkness rather than light." Why?

Erasmus, recognized by all as a reformer, did his work by the publication of the New Testament in Greek. "The work was undertaken in the interests of a purer Christianity." "It is my desire," he said, "to lead back that cold dispute about words called theology to its real fountain. Would to God that this work may bear as much fruit to Christianity as it has cost me toil and application." Here was a direct thrust at the study of dialectics in the universities. The meaningless disputes which constituted the course in theology was, by Erasmus, to be replaced by the living word of God. The Reformation drew nearer, and the papacy shuddered at the prospect.

Gradually the Spirit was returning, and this is seen more and more as we take up the life of Luther. The highway had been cleared by such forerunners as have already been mentioned.

"The fundamental principles of Protestantism are favorable to education," says Painter.[113]. "With the Scriptures and his conscience for guides, every man is elevated to the freedom and dignity of ordering his own religious life. The feeling of individual responsibility is awakened, and the spirit of inquiry fostered. Intelligence becomes a necessity. *The Bible must be studied; teachers must be provided; schools must be established.* Protestantism becomes the mother of popular education."

Again, the same author says: "It [Christianity] does not withdraw man from the ordinary callings and relations of life; it makes him a steward of God in the world, and exalts his daily labors in the household, in the schoolroom, in the workshop, on the farm, into a divine service. The Protestant view restores nature, as a subject of investigation, to its rights. The whole circle of knowledge—whatever is elevating, whatever prepares for useful living—is held in honor. *Primary and secondary schools* are encouraged; the best methods of instruction, based upon a study of man's nature and not upon the interests of the church, are sought out. Protestantism is a friend of universal learning." One French scholar says: "The Reformation contracted the obligation of placing everyone in a condition to save himself by reading and studying the Bible. Instruction became then the first of the duties of charity; and all who had charge of souls, from the father of a family to the sovereign of the state, were called upon... to favor popular education."[114]

It is no wonder, then, that much of Luther's time and ambition was spent in the cause of education. "The necessities of the Reformation gave Luther," says Painter, "an intense interest in education. The schools of the time, already inadequate in number and defective in method, were crippled during the early stages of the Reformation by the excited and unsettled condition of society. A new generation was growing up without education. *The establishment of schools became a necessary measure for the success and permanence of the Reformation.* The appeal had been made to the Word of God, and it was necessary to teach the masses to read it. Preachers and teachers were needed for the promulgation and defense of the gospel....As early as 1524, Luther made an appeal of marvelous energy to the authorities of the German cities for the establishment of schools. If we consider its pioneer character, in connection with its statement of principles and admirable recommendations, the address must be regarded the most important educational treatise ever written."[115] God had trained him for his position.

Here are the words of the Reformer. Judge for yourselves if they should not voice the sentiment of every true Protestant today! "He wrote," says D'Aubigné, "to the councilors of all the cities of Germany, calling upon them to found Christian schools." "Dear sirs," said Luther, "we annually expend so much money on arquebuses, roads, and dikes, why should we not spend a little to give one or two schoolmasters to our poor children? God stands at the door and knocks; blessed are we if we open to Him! Now the Word of God abounds. O my dear Germans, buy, buy, while the market is open before your houses. The Word of God and His grace are like a shower that falls and passes away. It was among the Jews; but it passed away, and now they have it no longer. Paul carried it into Greece; but in that country also it has passed away, and the Turk reigns there now. It came to Rome and the Latin empire; but there also it has passed away, and Rome now has the pope. O Germans, do not expect to have this Word forever. The contempt that is shown to it will drive it away. For this reason, let him who desires to possess it lay hold of it and keep it.

"Busy yourselves with the children; for many parents are like ostriches, they are hardened toward their little ones, and, satisfied with having laid the egg, they care nothing for it afterward....The true wealth of a city, its safety, and its strength, is to have many learned, serious, worthy, well-educated citizens. And whom must we blame, because there are so few at present, except your magistrates who have allowed your youth to grow up like trees in a forest?"[116]

D'Aubigné says truly: "It was not the public worship alone that the Reformation was ordained to change. The school was early placed beside the church, and these two great institutions, so powerful to regenerate the nations, were equally reanimated by it. *It was by a close alliance with learning that the Reformation entered into the world; in the hour of its triumph it did not forget its ally.*"[117] Luther "felt that to strengthen the Reformation it was requisite to work on the young, to improve the schools, and to propagate throughout Christendom the knowledge necessary for a profound study of the Holy Scriptures. This was one of the results."[118]

Painter, describing the educational work of the great Reformer, says: "With Luther, education was not an end in itself, but a means to more effective service in church and state. If people or rulers neglect the education of the young, they inflict an injury upon both the church and state; *they become* enemies of God and man; they advance the cause of Satan, and bring down upon themselves the curse of heaven. This is the fundamental thought that underlies all Luther's writings upon education."[119]

Luther expresses his views briefly in these words: "The common man does not think that he is under obligation to God and the world to send his son to school. Everyone thinks that he is free to bring up his son as he pleases, no matter what becomes of God's word and command. Yea, even our rulers act as if they were exempt from the divine command. No one thinks that God has earnestly willed and commanded that children be brought up to his praise and work—a thing that cannot be done without schools. On the contrary, *everyone hastens with his children after worldly gain.*"[120]

Luther's words ringing down the centuries must be echoed by all true Protestants today. Where are the men with the courage of educational reformers?

"Luther did not concern himself about the education of the clergy only, it was his desire that knowledge should not be confined to the church; he proposed extending it to the laity, who hitherto had been deprived of it....He emancipated learning from the hands of the priests, who had monopolized it, like those of Egypt in times of old, and put it within the reach of all."[121] Luther grasped with wonderful clearness the real meaning of Christian education, and there is scarcely a phase of it which he has left untouched.

"If we survey," says Dittes, "the pedagogy of Luther in all its extent, and imagine it fully realized in practice, what a splendid picture the schools and education of the sixteenth century would present! We should have courses of study, textbooks, teachers, methods, principles, and modes of discipline, schools and school regulations, that could serve as models for our own age."

The Reformer writes: "Where would preachers, lawyers, and physicians come from if the liberal arts were not taught? From this source must they all come. This, I say, no one can ever sufficiently remunerate the industrious and pious teacher that faithfully educates....Yet people shamefully despise this calling among us, as if it were nothing, and at the same time they pretend to be Christians! If I were obliged to leave off preaching and other duties, there is no office I would rather have than that of school-teacher; for I know that this work is, with preaching, the most useful, greatest, and best; and I do not know which of the two is to be preferred.

For it is difficult to make old dogs docile, and old rogues pious, yet that is what the ministry works at, and must work at in great part, in vain; but young trees, although some may break, are more easily bent and trained. Therefore, let it be one of *the highest virtues on earth faithfully to educate the children of others who neglect it themselves.*"[122]

Germany was aroused. "In 1525 he was commissioned by the Duke of Mansfield to establish two schools in his native town;... one for the primary and the other for secondary instruction." They were not conducted after the manner of papal schools, differing only in the fact that the teacher was a Protestant. "Both in the course of study and in the methods of instruction these schools become models after which many others were fashioned....In a few years the Protestant portion of Germany was supplied with schools. They were still defective,... but, at the same time, they were greatly superior to any that had preceded them. Though no complete system of popular instruction was established, the foundation for it was laid. To this great result, Luther contributed more than any other man of his time; and *this fact makes him the leading educational reformer of the sixteenth century.*"[123]

The changes wrought by Luther were not mere superficial, formal changes; but as the Reformation, as a religious movement, struck a deathblow to the papacy, viewed as an educational movement, it is found to have cut directly across the established methods of popular education. It meant a change in the *courses*, a different idea of graduation, a change in *text-books*, in *methods of teaching, methods of study,* and *character of the teachers.*

He was perhaps the first of the reformers to recognize the value of nature study. He once said: "We are at the dawn of a new era; for we are beginning to recover the knowledge of the external world that we have lost since the fall of Adam. Erasmus is indifferent to it; he does not care to know how fruit is developed from the germ. But by the grace of God, we already recognize in the most delicate flower the wonders of divine goodness and the omnipotence of God. We see in His creatures the power of His word. He commanded, and the thing stood fast. See that force display itself in the stone of a peach. It is very hard, and the germ that it encloses is very tender; but, when the moment has come, the stone must open to let out the young plant that God calls into life."[124] It may at first seem strange that the bold, brave man who aroused the world by his theses nailed to the church door, should have a character to which the gentleness of nature made such a strong appeal. But Luther was a true preacher in that he was a teacher. What wonder that his work was enduring! It stands close beside the life-work of his Master, Jesus—the Teacher sent of God.

Before carrying the work of Luther further, it is neces-sary to introduce a new character, born, it would seem, at a moment when his special mental qualities were most needed and fitted by heaven to stand by Luther's side as an aid and as a comfort in the mighty storm through which he must pass. I refer to Melanchthon; God chose him as a *teacher*, and im-parted to him, in a wonderful degree, that gift of the Spirit. A few extracts from D'Aubigné will show clearly how he was guided into the paths of the Reformation, there to become one of the greatest workers for that cause.

He was born in 1497; hence, when Luther began his work in 1517, Melanchthon was a youth of twenty. "He was remark-able for the excellence of his understanding, and his facility in learning and explaining what he had learnt." "Melanchthon at twelve years of age went to the University of Heidelberg... and took his bachelor's degree at fourteen." "In 1512, Reuch-lin [the reformer referred to on a previous page] invited him to Tubingen....The Holy Scriptures especially engaged his at-tention....Rejecting the empty systems of the schoolmen, he adhered to the plain word of the gospel."[125]

Erasmus wrote: "I entertain the most distinguished and splendid expectations of Melanchthon. God grant that this young man may long survive us. He will entirely eclipse Erasmus."

"In 1514 he was made doctor of philosophy, and then began to teach. He was seventeen years old. The grace and charm that he imparted to his lessons formed the most striking contrast to the tasteless method which the doctors, and above all, the monks, had pursued till then."

Frederick applied to Erasmus and Reuchlin for an instruc-tor for the University of Wittenberg. Melanchthon was recom-mended. Reaching the university, he did not make the most favorable impression on Luther and other professors, "when they saw his youth, his shyness, and diffident manners." After his opening address, however, Luther and others became his ardent admirers. Luther wrote: "I ask for no other Greek master. But I fear that his delicate frame will be unable to support our mode of living, and that we shall be unable to keep him long on account of the smallness of his salary."

The spirit of Christianity and of Christian education had drawn two souls together, and the success of the work from this time on depended largely upon this union. Says D'Aubigné: "Melanchthon was able to respond to Luther's affection. He soon found in him a kindness of disposition, a strength of mind, a courage, a discretion, that he had never found till then in any man....We cannot too much admire the goodness and wisdom of God in bringing together two men so different, and yet so necessary to one another. Luther possessed warmth, vigor, and strength; Melanchthon clearness, discretion, and mildness. Luther gave energy to Melanchthon; Melanchthon moderated Luther. They were like substances in a state of positive and negative electricity, which mutually act upon each other. If Luther had been without Melanchthon, perhaps the torrent would have overflowed its banks; Melanchthon, when Luther was taken from him by death, hesitated, and gave way, even where he should not have yielded."

Should you question why I thus dwell upon the life and character of Melanchthon, I reply, Because from this union of two souls flowed the great educational reform of the sixteenth century. The two did what neither could have done alone; and the study of their lives alone reveals the secret of success in Christian education today.

It was a notable day to Wittenberg when Melanchthon arrived. "The barrenness that scholasticism had cast over education was at an end. A new manner of teaching and of studying began with Melanchthon. 'Thanks to him,' says an illustrious German historian, 'Wittenberg became the school of the nation.' "

"The zeal of the teachers [Luther and Melanchthon] was soon communicated to the disciples. It was decided to reform the method of instruction. With the electors' consent, certain courses that possessed merely scholastic importance were suppressed; and at the same time the study of the classics received a fresh impulse. [Remember, however, that this study of the classics was the Greek and Hebrew Scriptures.] The school at Wittenberg was transformed, and the contrast with other universities became daily more striking."[126]

The results of these changes were no less marvelous than the changes themselves. The author last quoted says: Wittenberg "flourished daily more and more, and was eclipsing all the other schools. A crowd of students flocked thither from all parts of Germany to hear this extraordinary man, whose teaching appeared to open a new era in religion and learning. These youths, who came from every province, halted as soon as they discovered the steeples of Wittenberg in the distance; they raised their hands to heaven, and praised God for having caused the light of truth to shine forth from this city, as from Zion in times of old, and whence it spread even to the most distant countries. A life and activity, till then unknown, animated the university."

Such a school did not call together a class of students careless in habit and listless in study; for the fare, as before noted, was meager, and there was no great outward display. Those who attended came seeking for truth; and as their souls were filled with spiritual meat, they returned to their homes, "even to the most distant countries," to spread the truths of Christian education. Luther himself wrote: "Our students here are as busy as ants." Two thousand students from all parts of Europe thronged the lecture room of Melanchthon."

The life and work of those two animating spirits at Wittenberg cannot be measured by any earthly standard. Melanchthon said: "I apply myself solely to one thing, the defense of letters. By our example we must excite youth to the admiration of learning, and induce them to love it for its own sake, and not for the advantage that they may derive from it. The destruction of learning brings with it the ruin of everything that is good—religion, morals, and all things human and divine. The better a man is, the greater his ardor in the preservation of learning; for he knows that, of all plagues, ignorance is the most pernicious." "To neglect the young in our schools is just like taking the spring out of the year. They, indeed, take away the spring from the year who permit the schools to decline, because religion cannot be maintained without them."

Luther had stated that a reform in methods and courses was necessary. Melanchthon had assisted in that work.

He did still more. Breaking away as they did from the educational system of the universities of the world, and basing instruction upon the Word of God, it became necessary to have new text-books. Melanchthon applied himself with great diligence to this duty. He was an arduous student, often arising at three in the morning, and many of his works were written between that hour and the dawn. Besides his Greek and Latin grammars, he is the author of works on logic, rhetoric, physics, and ethics. "These works, written in a clear and scientific form, soon became popular, and some of them held their place in the schools for more than a hundred years."

The study of theology had been degraded into the pursuit of subtle arguments and idle controversies. Melanchthon wrote a work on dogmatic theology, publishing it in 1521. Of this work, Luther wrote: "Whoever wishes to become a theologian now enjoys great advantages; for, first of all, he has the *Bible*, which is so clear that he can read it without difficulty. Then let him read in addition the Loci Communes of Melanchthon....If he has these two things, he is a theologian from whom neither the devil nor heretics shall be able to take away anything."

Melanchthon's life was not devoted alone to the education of such students as could attend Wittenberg, nor were his changes of the educational system applicable only to the higher schools and universities. Stump says: "Amid all the distractions and anxieties of this period, Melanchthon steadily directed his efforts to the advancement of education and the building up of good Christian schools. During a period covering many years, he found time, in spite of his numerous other engagements, to give elementary instruction to a number of young men who lived with him in his own house. He did this on account of the lamentable lack of suitable preparatory schools. He lost no opportunity, however, to provide for this lack, whenever he found it possible to do so.

"In the spring of 1525, with Luther's help, he reorganized the schools of Eisleben and Magdeburg. He went to Nuremberg, and assisted in the establishment of a gymnasium [high school] in that city; and in the following spring he returned to Nuremberg, and formally opened the school. He delivered an address in Latin, in which he dwelt upon the importance of education, and the credit which the movers in this enterprise deserved. He declared that... *'the cause of true education is the cause of God.'* "[127]

Both church schools and higher schools, those offering instruction for students preparing for the universities, were organized by Melanchthon.

This work was not allowed to proceed without some bitter attacks from the schoolmen and representatives of papal education. For illustration of this fact, we have the words of D'Aubigné: "The schools, which for five centuries past had domineered over Christendom, far from giving way at the first blow of the Reformer [Luther], rose up haughtily to crush the man who dared pour out upon them the flood of his contempt." "Doctor Eck, the celebrated professor of Ingolstadt,... was a doctor of the schools and not of the Bible; well versed in the scholastic writings, but not in the Word of God....Eck represented the schoolmen." "Eck was a far more formidable adversary than Tetzel [the vender of indulgences], Prierio, or Hochstraten; the more his work surpassed theirs in learning and in subtlety, the more dangerous it was."[128] Thus Luther's most bitter enemies were those who had once been his warm friends, and those who offered the strongest opposition to his work were the teachers in the universities of Germany.

Luther was sometimes almost overcome in spirit by the ingratitude shown, and of Doctor Eck he once wrote: "If I did not know Satan's thoughts, I should be astonished at the fury which has led this man to break off so sweet and so new a friendship, and that, too, without warning me, without writing to me, without saying a single word."

It was in order to meet the opposition offered by the school men, and to put the Reformation on a firm basis, that Luther and Melanchthon formulated the Saxony school plan, and reorganized the German schools.

Stump says: "In the year 1527, Melanchthon took part with Luther in the visitation of the schools and churches of Saxony. It was high time for such a step. Affairs were in a wretched condition. In many places no religious instruction was given at all, because there were either no pastors and teachers stationed there, or those who were stationed there were grossly ignorant themselves. The greatest disorder imaginable reigned nearly everywhere....The financial condition of many of the churches was equally bad....It was the object of the visitation to bring order out of this chaos. Melanchthon was charged with making a beginning in Thuringia. The spiritual distress which he discovered rent his heart, and he often went aside, and wept over what he saw." "In 1528 Melanchthon drew up the 'Saxony school plan,' which served as the basis of organization for many schools throughout Germany."

According to this plan, teachers were to avoid "burdening the children with a *multiplicity of studies* that were not only unfruitful, but even hurtful." Again, "The teacher should not burden the children with too many books," and "it is necessary that the children be divided into classes." "Three classes, or grades, are recommended," and the subjects taught should be adapted to the age and condition of the pupil. Thus, avoid too many studies for children and youth; do not put too many books into their hands; group them according to their ability. This "plan" seems to resist the cramming system so universally followed today almost as vigorously as it opposed the papal schools of the sixteenth century.

A great work was set on foot—a revolution which was to affect the ages which followed. In the brief space of one man's life, plans were laid, *especially in the educational work,* which, if carried out by his successors, would have placed Germany in a position to rule the world. Instead of returning to the pit from which she had been dug, her schools and universities might have been models worthy of imitation throughout Europe and in America. Luther died, and Melanchthon, his co-laborer, was unable to carry forward the work. Theologians, pastors, ministers, into whose hands the work of the Reformation rightfully fell, *instead of multiplying Christian schools,* and carrying to perfection the methods of instruction introduced by Luther and Melanchthon, *passed by the greatest work of the age,* and by internal strifes and theological disputes lost the hard-won battle. The seeds of truth had been sown in *republicanism* and *Protestantism,* and these two institutions should have been held in Germany. *Education—Christian education—* alone could hold them there. This was neglected; and as lost children, the two went hand in hand to the Netherlands, to England, and finally to America, in search of a fostering mother—a pure system of education. The spirit and life so manifest in the teaching of the great Reformers, passed on, leaving Europe with the *form.* A house empty, swept, and garnished does not long so remain. The form was occupied by the spirit of the papacy, and Europe relapsed into a position from which she can be reclaimed only by a renewal of the plans of the sixteenth-century Reformers—a system of Christian education.

Chapter XIII
The Reaction After the Educational Reformation

THE most momentous event of the world's history, excepting alone the birth of the Redeemer, was the Reformation of the sixteenth century. Great religious movements have occurred before and since, but they are eclipsed by the brilliancy and far-reaching results of this one. More men have been reached, more lives revolutionized, than by the combined forces of all changes in civil and domestic circles since that time. The fact is, that when the causes of political changes in the modern world are considered, it must be acknowledged by every candid thinker that these changes are due in one way or another to the attitude assumed by the people concerned toward that one Reformation which was set in motion by the Wittenberg monk. Christ had been forgotten, and He came before the world again in the days of Luther.

A few quotations from Ranke show how far the Reformation extended in the brief space of forty years; and since we are dealing with the causes of this rapid spread, it is gratifying to see that this author gives in the most natural way due credit to the influence of the schools. Two things, then, should be noticed in reading these selections; first, the extent of territory covered by Protestant principles; second, the part played by schools and teachers in the conversion of nations. It is about the year 1563.

"In the *Scandinavian realms* they [the Protestants] had established themselves the more impregnably, because there their introduction was coincident with the establishment of new dynasties, and the remodeling of all political institutions. From the very first they were hailed with joy, as though there was in their nature a primitive affinity to the national feelings."

"In the year 1552, the last representatives of Catholicism in *Iceland* succumbed."

"On the southern shores, too, of the *Baltic*. Lutheranism had achieved complete predominance, at least among the population of German tongue."

In *Poland* it was said, "A Polish nobleman is not subject to the king; is he to be so to the pope?"

In *Hungary*, "Ferdinand I could never force the diet to any resolutions unfavorable to Protestantism."

"Protestantism not only reigned paramount in *northern Germany*, where it had originated, and in those districts of upper Germany where it had always maintained itself, but its grasp had been extended much more widely in every direction."

"In *Wurzburg and Bamberg* by far the greater part of the nobility and the episcopal functionaries, the magistrates and the burghers of the towns, at least the majority of them, and the bulk of the rural population, had passed over to the reforming party."

In *Bavaria* "the great majority of the nobility had adopted the Protestant doctrine, and a considerable portion of the towns was decidedly inclined to it."

"Far more than this, however, had been done in *Austria*. The *nobility of that country studied in Wittenberg; all the colleges of the land were filled with Protestants.*"

We are not surprised, therefore, to read that "it was said to be ascertained that not more, perhaps, than the thirtieth part of the population remained Catholic: *step by step, a national constitution unfolded itself, formed upon the principles of Protestantism.*" "In the *Rauris*, and the *Gastein*, in *St. Veit, Tamsweg*, and *Radstadt*, the inhabitants loudly demanded the sacramental cup, and this being refused [in order to compel them to remain Catholic], they ceased altogether to attend the sacrament. *They withheld their children, too, from the* [Catholic] *schools.*"

"The *Rhenish nobility* had early embraced Protestantism....In all the towns there existed already a Protestant party....*The inhabitants of Maniz, too, did not hesitate to send their children* to Protestant schools. In short, from west to east, and from north to south, throughout all Germany, Protestantism had unquestionably the preponderance."

"The Protestant notions extended their vivifying energies to the most remote and most forgotten corners of Europe. What an immense domain had they conquered within the space of forty years. From Iceland to the Pyrenees, from Finland to the heights of the Italian Alps. Even beyond the latter mountains opinions analogous had once, as we are aware, prevailed. *Protestantism embraced the whole range of the Latin church.* It had laid hold of a vast majority of the higher classes, and of the minds that took part in public life; whole nations clung to it with enthusiasm, and states had been remodeled by it. This is the more deserving of our wonder, inasmuch as Protestantism was by no means a mere antithesis, a negation of the papacy, or an emancipation from its rule; it was in the highest degree positive, a renovation of Christian notions and principles, that sway human life even to the profoundest mysteries of the soul."[129] Notice again that this was due to the educational ideas propagated by Protestants, and the reason why the papacy was so fast losing its foothold was because it had not yet learned that this Reformation, *which began in schools, and was carried forward by Christian schools, must be defeated in schools and by teachers.* For forty years Protestants had the right of way in education, and the results were stupendous.

Ranke says: "Protestant opinions had triumphed in the universities and educational establishments. Those old champions of Catholicism [the teachers] who had withstood Luther were dead, or in advanced years: young men capable of supplying their places had not yet arisen. Twenty years had elapsed in Vienna *since a single student of the university* had taken priest's orders. Even in Ingolstadt, pre-eminently Catholic as it was, *no competent candidates of the faculty of theology presented themselves to fill the places that had hitherto been always occupied by ecclesiastics.* The city of Cologne founded an endowed school; but when all the arrangements for it had been made, it was found that the regent was a Protestant. Cardinal Otto Truchess established a new university in his city of Dilligen, *with the express design of resisting the progress of Protestantism.* The credit of this institution was maintained for some years by a few distinguished Spanish theologians; but as soon as these left it, not a single scholar could be found in all Germany to succeed to their places, and even these were likewise filled with Protestants. About this period the teachers in Germany were all, almost without exception, Protestants. The whole body of the rising generation sat at their feet, and imbibed a hatred of the pope with the first rudiments of learning."[130]

Stress is not laid on their hatred of the pope, but on the fact that the rising generation sat at the feet of Protestant teachers throughout Germany; that parents withheld their children from the papal school, even though it might be necessary in so doing to send them from home to be educated; and finally, that the papacy was dying, and Protestantism was spreading through the work of the schools. Would that those schools might have retained their pristine purity and simplicity. No power on earth could then have retarded the progress of Protestantism, and instead of only modifying the history of many countries, it would eventually have swept from the earth all forms of tyranny, both civil and religious, for it breathed the freedom of the gospel and no oppression could stand before it. It is as impossible to withstand pure Christian education as it is to withstand Christ, whose power is its life and strength.

It is with a pang that one is forced to trace in this movement that oft-repeated chapter in the history of mankind. As the leader of Israel was allowed to view the promised land from the top of Pisgah, but must there lay aside his armor and sleep the sleep of death because of a departure from right principles, so Protestantism, through its schools, looked across Jordan, but failed to maintain the principle of faith which could at the crucial moment command the waters to part.

One reason for the decline is thus stated by Painter: "In their efforts to give Christian doctrine a scientific form [that is, to formulate it], *they lost its spirit. Losing its early freedom and life, Protestantism degenerated in a large measure into what has been called* 'dead orthodoxy'.... *Christian life* counted for little, and the Protestant world broke up into opposing factions. Says Kurtz, who is disposed to apologize for this period as far as possible: 'Like medieval scholasticism, in its concern for logic, theology almost lost vitality. Orthodoxy degenerated into orthodoxism; *externally,* not only discerning essential diversities, but disregarding the broad basis of a common faith, and running into odious and unrestrained controversy; *internally, holding to the form* of pure doctrine, but neglecting cordially to embrace it and to live consistently with it.' "[131]

How narrow the line between truth and error! How easy for those who had been given to eat of the tree of life to turn to the tree of knowledge of good and evil! What a pity that Protestant educators could not remain true to their trust! When on the eve of success, they turned to the old paths, and "called into existence a dialectic scholasticism which was in no way inferior to that of the most flourishing period of the Middle Ages."[132] Papal principles are papal, whether advocated by Catholics or Protestants; having left the fountain of the pure waters of faith, they turned to the only other accessible source of knowledge—the pagan world. That system of education introduced by Luther and Melanchthon, founded upon the *Holy Scriptures*, and through them viewing the sciences, mathematics, and literature, using the latter only as a means of illustrating God's Word, was replaced by the *scholasticism of the Middle Ages.* One involuntarily asks, "How many times, O Israel, wilt thou return into Egypt?"

This decline is described in the following quotations taken from Painter, and they need no comment: "During the period extending from the middle of the sixteenth to the beginning of the eighteenth century, three leading tendencies are apparent in education. These may be characterized as the theological, the humanistic, and the practical....A large share of the intellectual strength of the age was turned to theology. Every phase of religious truth, particularly in its doctrinal and speculative aspects, was brought under investigation. Theology was elevated to a science, and doctrinal systems were developed with logical precision, and *extended to trifling subtilities.*"[133]

In the figure of the Bible they strained for gnats, meanwhile swallowing the camel. The life was thus lost in the pulpit and in the theological schools. It was again the "teaching for doctrines the commandments of men."

Painter further says "The schools, which stand in close relation to religion, were naturally influenced in a large measure by the theological tendencies of the age. Theological interests imposed upon the schools *a narrow range of subjects, a mechanical method of instruction,* and a cruel discipline. The principle of authority, *exacting* a blind submission of the pupil, prevailed in the schools of every grade. The young were regarded not as tender plants to be carefully nurtured and developed, but as untamed animals to be repressed or broken."[134]

Notice the creeping in of those very characteristics of papal education so often referred to heretofore: 1, narrow range of subjects; 2, mechanical instruction—memory work devoid of understanding; 3, arbitrary government, as seen in the matter of discipline. To this we must add that which is the natural accompaniment in papal instruction—the teaching of Latin. Says Painter, quoting Dittes: " 'In the higher institutions, and even in the wretched town schools, Latin was the Moloch to which countless minds fell an offering in return for the blessing granted to a few. *A dead knowledge of words took the place of a living knowledge of things.* Latin schoolbooks supplanted the book of nature, the book of life, the book of mankind. And in the popular schools, youthful minds were tortured over the spelling book and catechism. The method of teaching was almost everywhere, in the primary as well as in the higher schools, a mechanical and compulsory drill in unintelligible formulas. The pupils were obliged to learn, *but they were not educated to see and hear, to think and prove,* and were not led to a true independence and personal perfection. The teachers found their function in teaching the prescribed text, not in harmoniously developing the young human being according to the laws of nature—a process, moreover, that lay under the ban of ecclesiastical orthodoxy.' "[135]

That there was a cramming process followed equal to any twentieth-century school, is evident. "The discipline answered to the content and spirit of the instruction....The principle was to tame the pupils, not to educate them. They were to hold themselves motionless, that the school exercises might not be disturbed. What took place in their minds, and how their several characters were constituted, the school pedants did not understand and appreciate."

In order to appreciate the rapidity with which the relapse took place from the educational system introduced by Luther to the medieval principles and methods, our attention is directed to the school of John Sturm. This man, "regarded as the greatest educator that the Reformed Church produced during this period," died in 1589, less than seventy years after the Diet of Worms; hence his work fell within the half century following those forty years of unusual prosperity for Protestantism which has already been noticed. His work is contemporary with the first Jesuit school of Germany. The decline is visible in every feature of his work.

John Sturm presided for forty years over the gymnasium of Strasburg, and his boast was that his institution "reproduced the best periods of Athens and Rome; and, in fact, he succeeded in giving to his adopted city the name of New Athens." Sturm's school stood as a halfway mark between the Christian schools and the purely papal schools of the Jesuits, but since compromise always places a person or institution on the side of wrong, in weighing the worth of his school the balances necessarily tip in favor of the papacy.

That his was a mixture of the medieval classical literature with a thin slice of Scripture sandwiched in for effect, is seen in the course of study as outlined by Painter. The school was divided into ten classes covering ten years, but only so much is given as is necessary to show the character of the studies: "Tenth class—The alphabet, reading, writing, Latin declensions and conjugations, German or Latin catechism." "Ninth class—Latin declensions and conjugations continued. Memorizing of Latin words." The eighth and the seventh classes are about the same. In the sixth, Greek is begun. The fifth class is as follows: "Study of words,… versification, mythology, Cicero, and Virgil's eclogues, Greek vocabulary. On Saturday and Sunday, one of Paul's epistles."[136] The remaining four classes have much "learning by heart," rhetoric, Paul's epistles, orations of Demosthenes, the Iliad of Odyssey; memorizing and recitation of the Epistle to the Romans, dialectics, and rhetoric continued; Virgil, Horace, Homer, Thucydides, Sallust, weekly dramatic entertainments, and again a reading of Paul's epistles.

Such a course of instruction was well fitted to bridge the gulf between the papacy and Protestantism. It was imbibing perhaps unconsciously the spirit of the new papal schools. "History, mathematics, natural science, and the mother tongue are ignored. A great gap is left between the gymnasium and life—a gap that could not be filled even by the university. In aiming to reproduce Greece and Rome in the midst of modern Christian civilization, Sturm's scheme involves a *vast anachronism.*"[137]

The Strasburg gymnasium at one time numbered several thousand pupils representing Denmark, Poland, Portugal, France, and England. "Sturm's influence extended to *England, and thence to America.*" An English writer says: "No one who is acquainted with the education given at our principal classical schools, *Eaton, Winchester*, and *Westminster*, forty years ago, can fail to see that their curriculum was framed in a great degree on Sturm's model."[138] And yet it is acknowledged that his "scheme involves a *vast anachronism.*" To show that Sturm is the father of much of the instruction now given in our high schools and universities, Rosenkranz says: "John Sturm, of Strasburg, long before Comenius, had laid the foundation of what has become the *traditional course of instruction and methods of study in the classical schools for preparation for college.*"[139] The decline in the matter of instruction was accompanied by a corresponding retrogression in the morals of university students. Painter tells us that "the state of morals at the universities of the sixteenth and seventeenth centuries was very low. Idleness, drunkenness, disorder, and licentiousness prevailed in an unparalleled degree. The practice of *hazing* was universal, and new students were subjected to shocking indignities." Duke Albrecht, of the university of Jena, wrote in 1624: " 'Customs before unheard of, inexcusable, unreasonable, and wholly barbarian, have come into existence.' " Then he speaks of the insulting names, the expensive suppers, and the carousing of the students, until " 'parents in distant places either determine not to send their children to this university... or to take them away again.' "[140]

Protestantism lost much because she ceased to educate her children. Had Protestantism remained true to her first principles of education, her overthrow would have been impossible. She paved the way for her own fall by departing gradually from the gospel, and by leaning more and more toward the classics and scholasticism. It was this decline on her own part, caused by the insidious workings of the Jesuits, which made possible the great victories of this order in later years. It was when Rome saw her youth slipping from her hands into the Protestant schools, and as a result, a few years later, found whole nations refusing obedience, and building for themselves new forms of government, that, in her distress, she grasped the offer made by *Loyola*. And while the power he represented in its organization, placed itself above the pope, becoming, as it were, *a papacy of the papacy,* still she accepted his offer, and the *counter educational move* began. The Jesuits organized to combat reformation in educational lines. In speaking of the Jesuits, Painter says: "This order, established by Ignatius Loyola [in 1534], found its special mission in combating the Reformation. As the most effective means of arresting the progress of Protestantism, it aimed at controlling education, particularly among the wealthy and the noble. In rivalry with the schools of Protestant countries, it developed an immense educational activity, and earned for its schools a great reputation." Again, the same writer says "More than any other agency it stayed the progress of the Reformation, and it even succeeded in winning back territory already conquered by Protestantism. Although employing the pulpit and the confessional, it *worked chiefly through its schools, of which it established and controlled large numbers.* Education in all Catholic countries gradually passed into its hands." In order to understand the reason for the success of the Jesuits as teachers it is necessary to glance at the plan of studies prepared in 1588 from a draft made by Loyola himself. "Every member of the order," says Painter, "became a *competent and practical teacher.* He received a thorough course in the ancient classics, philosophy, and theology. During the progress of his later studies he was

required to teach." Jesuit schools contained two courses, the lower corresponding very closely to the work of
Sturm. Rosenkranz gives an excellent description of the
educational system of the Jesuits. He says:—

"In instruction they developed so exact a mechanism
that they gained the reputation of having model school
regulations, and even Protestants sent their children to
them. From the close of the sixteenth century to the present time they have based their teaching upon the *Ratio et
institutio studiorum Societatis Jesu* of Claudius of Aqua-
viva. Following that, they distinguished two courses of
teaching, a higher and a lower. The lower included nothing but an external knowledge of the Latin language, and
some fortuitous knowledge of history, of antiquities, and
of mythology. *The memory was cultivated as a means of
keeping down free activity of thought and clearness of
judgment.* The higher course comprehended dialectics,
rhetoric, physics, and morals. Dialectics was expounded
as the art of sophistry. In rhetoric, they favored the po-
lemical and emphatic style of the African fathers of the
church and their gorgeous phraseology; in physics, they
followed Aristotle closely, and especially encouraged
reading of the books 'De Generatione et Corruptione'
and 'De Coelo,' on which they commented after their
fashion; finally, in morals, casuistic skepticism was their
central point. They made much of rhetoric, on account
of their sermons, giving to it careful attention. They laid
stress on declamation, and introduced it into their showy
public examinations through the performance of Latin
school comedies, and thus amused the public, disposed
them to approval, and at the same time quite innocently
practiced the pupil in the art of assuming a feigned character.

"Diplomatic conduct was made necessary to the pupils of the Jesuits, as well by their strict military discipline as by their system of mutual distrust, espionage,
and informing. Implicit obedience relieved the pupils

from all responsibility as to the moral justification of their deeds. This exact following out of all commands and refraining from any criticism as to principles, created a moral indifference; and, from the necessity of having consideration for the peculiarities and caprices of the superior on whom all others were dependent, arose eye service. The coolness of mutual distrust sprang from the necessity which each felt of being on his guard against every other as a talebearer. The most deliberate hypocrisy and pleasure in intrigue merely for the sake of intrigue—this subtlest poison of moral corruption—were the result. Jesuitism had not only an interest in the material profit, which, when it had corrupted souls, fell to its share, but it also had an interest in the educative process of corruption. With absolute indifference as to the idea of morality...or the moral quality of the means used to attain its end, it rejoiced in the efficacy of secrecy, and the accomplished and calculating understanding, and in deceiving the credulous by means of its graceful, seemingly scrupulous, moral language."[141]

Here is a picture of *this papacy of the papacy.* Again, I say, had Protestantism remained true to principle, even this system could not have accomplished its overthrow; but since truth was neglected by Protestant schools, this system of the Jesuits easily carried every country into which it was introduced. "The Jesuit system of education... was intended to meet the active influence of Protestantism in education. It was remarkably successful, and for a century [following 1584] nearly all the foremost men of Christendom came from Jesuit schools. In 1710 they had six hundred and twelve colleges, one hundred and fifty-seven normal schools, twenty-four universities, and an immense number of lower schools. These schools laid very great stress on *emulation.* Their experiments in this principle are so extensive and long-continued that they furnish a most valuable phase in the history of pedagogy in this respect alone. In the matter of supervision, they are also worthy of study. They had a fivefold system, each subordinate being obedient to his superior. Besides this, there was a complete system of espionage on the part of the teachers and pupil monitors."[142]

On the subject of emulation, as made use of in the schools of the Jesuits, Painter gives us these thoughts: "The Jesuits made much of emulation, and in their eager desire to promote it they adopted means that could not fail to excite jealousy and envy. Says the Plan of Studies: 'He who knows how to excite emulation has found the most powerful auxiliary in his teaching. Let the teacher, then, highly appreciate this valuable aid, and let him study to make the wisest use of it. Emulation awakens and develops all the powers of man. In order to maintain emulation, it will be necessary that each pupil have a rival to control his conduct and criticize him; also, magistrates, questors, censors, and decurions should be appointed among the students. Nothing will be held more honorable than to outstrip a fellow student, and nothing more dishonorable than to be outstripped. Prizes will be distributed to the best pupils with the greatest possible solemnity. Out of school the place of honor will everywhere be given to the most distinguished pupils.' "[143]

As the Colossus of Rhodes stood astride the Greek waters, so the Jesuit schools spanned the gulf of education. One foot stood in Greece amidst its classics (for "Aristotle furnished the leading text-books"), the other on Christian soil, having the *form* of godliness; but like the demigods of Greece, it was neither human nor divine. The results of the educational system of the Jesuits are well summed up in another paragraph from Painter:—

"The Jesuit system of education, based not upon a study of man, but upon the interests of the order, was necessarily narrow. It sought showy results with which to dazzle the world. A well-rounded development was nothing. The principle of authority, suppressing all freedom and independence of thought, prevailed from beginning to end.

Religious pride and intolerance were fostered. While our baser feelings were highly stimulated, the nobler side of our nature was wholly neglected. Love of country, fidelity to friends, nobleness of character, enthusiasm for beautiful ideals, were insidiously suppressed. For the rest, we adopt the language of Quick: 'The Jesuits did not aim at developing *all* the faculties of their pupils, but merely the receptive and reproductive faculties. When the young man had acquired a thorough mastery of the Latin language for all purposes; when he was well versed in the theological and philosophical opinions of his preceptors; when he was skillful in dispute, and could make a brilliant display from the resources of a well-stored memory, he had reached the highest points to which the Jesuits sought to lead him. Originality and independence of mind, love of truth for its own sake, the power of reflecting and of forming correct judgments, were not merely neglected, they were suppressed in the Jesuits' system. But in what they attempted they were eminently successful, and their success went a long way toward securing their popularity.' "[144]

One cannot condemn without reserve the Jesuitical system of education; for all false systems contain some points of truth, and the strength of all these systems lies in their close counterfeit of the true. Hence, we can agree with these words: "Whatever its defects as a system of general education, it was admirably suited to Jesuit purposes, and in some particulars, it embodied valuable principles." As the progress of the papacy through the Jesuitical schools is followed into one country and then another, one admires the constancy and self-sacrifice of those who have committed their lives to the order. Had Protestants been one half as diligent in advocating the principles of Christian education as the Jesuit teachers have been in counteracting the influence of the Reformation, far different results would today be seen in the world. In tracing the growth of the schools of the Jesuits we begin with Germany, the heart of the reform movement, and follow quite carefully the history as given by Ranke: "Bishop Urban became acquainted with Le Jay and heard from him, for the first time, of the *colleges* the *Jesuits had founded in several universities.*

"Upon this, the bishop advised his imperial master [Ferdinand I] to found a *similar college in Vienna*, seeing how great was the decay of Catholic theologian Germany. Ferdinand warmly embraced the suggestion; in a letter he wrote to Loyola on the subject, he declares his conviction that *the only means to uphold the declining cause of Catholicism in Germany, was to give the rising generation learned and pious Catholics for teachers.*" We can understand the grounds for this decision when we recall the statement that about 1563 it was said that "twenty years had elapsed in Vienna since a single student of the university had taken priest's orders." "The preliminaries," says Ranke, "were easily arranged. In the year 1551 thirteen Jesuits, among them Le Jay himself, arrived in Vienna, and were in the first instance, granted a dwelling, chapel, and pension, by Ferdinand, until shortly after he incorporated them with the university, and even assigned to them the visitation of it." "Soon after this they arose to consideration in *Cologne*," but for a time had little success. In 1556 the endowed school referred to before governed by a Protestant regent, "gave them an opportunity of gaining a firmer footing. For since there was a party in the city bent above all things on maintaining the Catholic character of the university, the advice given by the patrons of the Jesuits to hand over the establishment to that order, met with attention." "At the same period, they also gained a firm footing in *Ingolstadt*." "From these three metropolitan centers the Jesuits now spread out in every direction." These schools were, some of them at least, training schools for Catholic teachers; for Ranke tells of a certain man in Hungary, Olahus by name, and dedicated in infancy to the church, who, "contemplating the general decay of Catholicism in Hungary, saw that the last hope left for it was that of maintaining its hold on the common people, who had not yet wholly lapsed from its rule. To this end, however, there lacked teachers of Catholic principles, and to form whom, he founded a college of Jesuits at Tyrnau in the year 1561." "Two privy councilors of the elector Daniel, of Mainz... conceived likewise that the *admission of the Jesuits was the only means that promised a recovery of the University of Mainz.* In spite of the opposition made by the canons and feudal proprietors, they founded a college of the order in Mainz, and a preparatory school in Aschaffenburg."

The Jesuits advanced up the Rhine. "They particularly coveted a settlement at Spires, both because... there were so many distinguished men [assembled there] over whom it would be of extraordinary moment to possess influence; and also, in order to be placed near the Heidelberg University, which at that day enjoyed the highest repute for its Protestant professors. They gradually carried their point." It is interesting to note how they shadowed the Protestant schools, as if, like a parasite, to suck from them their life. "In order to bring back his University of Dillingen to its original purpose, Cardinal Truchess resolved to dismiss all the professors who still taught there, and to commit the establishment entirely to the Jesuits."

To show the rapidity with which the Jesuits worked, Ranke says: "In the year 1551 they had not yet any fixed position in Germany;" "in 1556 they had extended over Bavaria and the Tyrol, Franconia, and Swabia, a great part of Rhineland, and Austria, and they had penetrated into Hungary, Bohemia, and Moravia." True to the purpose of the order, "their labors were above all devoted to the universities. They were ambitious of rivaling the fame of those of the Protestants? "The Jesuits displayed no less assiduity in the conduct of their Latin schools. It was one of the leading maxims of Lainez that the lower grammatical classes should be supplied with good teachers, since first impressions exercise the greatest influence over the whole future life of the individual." The Jesuits were willing to devote a lifetime to one phase of education. "It was found that young persons learned more under them in half a year than with others in two years; even Protestants called back their children from distant schools, and put them under the care of the Jesuits." From this last sentence two things are to be observed. Protestants had lost sight of the importance of education, and their schools had greatly deteriorated, else they would not have entrusted their children to the Jesuits. While the Jesuits began by working into the universities, "schools for the poor, modes of instruction adapted for children, and catechizing followed." "The instruction of the Jesuits was conveyed wholly in the spirit of that enthusiastic devotion which had from the first so peculiarly characterized their order." This had its effect; for earnest, wholehearted work on the part of the teacher, even though the methods may be wrong and material false, will surely react in the lives of the pupils. Viewing the work of Jesuit teachers, one feels to exclaim, "Since thou art so noble, I would thou wert on our side!" And so "erelong the children, who frequented the schools of the Jesuits in Vienna, were distinguished for their resolute refusal to partake on fast days of forbidden meats which their parents ate."

Teachers had more weight with the children than the parents themselves, and became leaders of the older members of the family, so that "the feelings thus engendered in the schools were propagated throughout the mass of the population by preaching and confession."

The final results in Germany, Ranke gives thus: "They occupied the professors' chairs, and found pupils who attached themselves to their doctrines....*They conquered the Germans on their own soil, in their very home, and wrested from them a part of their native land.*"[145] So much for Germany and its Jesuit schools.

Concerning the capture of France by the Jesuits it is not necessary to say much. Ranke gives a few strong paragraphs, showing the work of the order as teachers.

The Protestants of France made a great mistake, and brought their cause into disrepute, especially in Paris, by taking up arms in a time of commotion, and Ranke says: "Backed by this state of public feeling, the Jesuits established themselves in France. They began there on a somewhat small scale, being constrained to content themselves with colleges thrown open to them by a few ecclesiastics....They encountered at first the most obstinate resistance in the great cities, especially in Paris,... but they at last forced their way through all impediments, and were admitted in the year 1564 to the privilege of teaching. Lyons had already received them. Whether it was the result of good fortune or of merit, they were enabled at once to produce some men of brilliant talents from amongst them....In Lyons, especially, the Huguenots were completely routed, their preachers exiled, their churches demolished, and their books burned; whilst, on the other hand, a splendid college was erected for the Jesuits in 1567. They had also a distinguished professor, whose exposition of the Bible attracted *crowds of charmed and attentive youth.* From these chief towns they now spread over the kingdom in every direction."[146] Through the influence gained as educators, 3,800 copies of Angler's Catechism were sold in the space of eight years in Pads alone. France no longer *leaned* toward Protestantism. She had been regained by the Jesuit schools.

Concerning the work in England, more is said, and our own connection with that kingdom adds weight in our eyes to the history of her education. Thompson says: "During the reign of Elizabeth the papal authorities renewed their exertions to put a stop to Protestantism in England, and sent more Jesuits there for that purpose."[147] What they could not accomplish through intrigue and civil policy they were more sure to gain through the schools; hence Thompson says: "They accomplished one thing, which was to carry away with them several young English noblemen, to be educated by the Jesuits in Flanders, so as to fit them for treason against their own country—repeating in this the experiment Loyola had made in Germany....The Jesuits endeavored to become the educators of English youths as they had those of Germany....The pope therefore established an English college at *Rome*, to educate young Englishmen."

Of this college, Ranke tells us further: "William Allen first conceived the idea of uniting the young English Catholics who resided on the continent for the prosecution of their studies, and, chiefly through the support of Pope Gregory, he established a college for them at Douay. This, however, did not seem to the pope to be adequate for the purpose in view. He wished to provide for those fugitives under his own eyes a more tranquil and less dangerous retreat than could be found in the disturbed Netherlands; accordingly, he founded an English college in Rome, and consigned it to the care of the Jesuits. No one was admitted into the college who did not pledge himself, on the completion of his studies, to return to England, and to preach there the faith of the Roman Church."[148]

America was settled when the Jesuit power was at its height. Those teachers who penetrated Germany without fear, and secretly stole into England when it was unsafe for them to be identified, followed closely the paths of discovery and settlement. "In the beginning of the seventeenth century we find," says Ranke, "the stately fabric of the Catholic Church in South America fully reared....The Jesuits taught grammar and the liberal arts, and a theological seminary was connected with their college of San Ildefonso. All branches of theological study were taught in the universities of Mexico and Lima."[149]

In North America, their vigilance was no less marked. "In 1611 Jesuit missionaries came over and labored with remarkable zeal and success in converting the Indians."[150] In Maryland, a Catholic colony from the first, they held unbounded sway. Speaking of the time of Lord Baltimore, Thompson says: "At that time, in England, the papists were

chiefly under the influence of the Jesuits, whose vigilance
was too sleepless to permit the opportunity of planting
their society in the New World to escape them."[151] Their
work has been quietly done from the very first, and some
think that because of the papal decree of 1773, suppressing the order, they have ceased their work. This, however,
is a mistake; for "Gregory XVI, whose pontificate commenced in 1831, was the first pope who seemed encouraged by the idea that the papacy would ultimately establish itself in the United States. His chief reliance, as the
means of realizing this hope, was upon the *Jesuits*, upon
whose entire devotion to the principles of absolutism he
could confidently rely."[152] But the Jesuits always accomplish their work largely by means of education, hence we
may look for them to use the same tactics in our country
that had proved so eminently successful to their cause in
England and Germany.

"The chief thing with the Jesuits, "as Gressinger
writes, "was to obtain the sole direction of education,
so that by getting the young into their hands, they could
fashion them after their own pattern." It has been the
avowed aim of the Jesuits to stamp out Protestantism,
and with this, republicanism. In this country, where these
two principles were pre-eminently conspicuous, and so
closely associated that whatever kills one kills the other,
it is doubly true that by gaining control of the educational
system the order could work for the papacy the utter ruin of
America, both from a religious and a civil standpoint. From
the dawn of our history there has been within our borders,
mingling with our loyal citizens, a class of educators who
carry out this principle described by Thompson. "The Roman Catholic youth are forbidden by the papal system from
accepting as true the principles of the Declaration of Independence or of the Constitution of the United States."[153]
Leo XIII, who was educated a Jesuit [Thompson], remains
true to his principles. His biographer says "that the 'false
education' and 'antichristian training' of the young which

prevail in the United States and among the liberal and progressive peoples of the world must be done away with, abandoned, and 'Thomas Aquinas [a Catholic of the thirteenth century] must once more be enthroned as the "angel of the schools;" his methods and doctrines must be the light of all higher teaching, for his works are only revealed truth set before the human mind in its most scientific form.' "[154]

It is unnecessary to state the number of schools established by Catholics in the United States, which have been placed under the control of the Jesuits; neither is it necessary to trace the attempts which have been made by the papacy, at irregular periods in our history, to obtain the control of our public school system. The affairs at Stillwater, Minn., and at Faribault, in the same state, while unsuccessful, were weather vanes showing the direction of the wind—were posers to test the public pulse, and just so surely show the policy of the papacy in educational matters. Of far greater importance to us as Protestants is the fact that *Jesuitical principles may and do prevail in our popular system of education,* and these principles, whether carried out by Jesuits, or by the ordinary teacher who is unconscious of her situation, and unmindful of the result of her methods, bring about the fall of Protestantism and republicanism. Our nation has repudiated her foundation principles; are our Protestant churches doing likewise? The history of the educational institutions of the United States, which are discussed in the next chapters, will show how the plan of work now followed in our universities, colleges, and schools of lower grades, are patterning after Sturm, and how they go farther back, connecting the twentieth century. with the scholasticism of the Middle Ages. It is without the slightest feelings of animosity toward the Jesuits or the papacy that these facts are traced. These both do for their cause what will best serve to upbuild it. Their methods, in so far as they accomplish their desired end, are to be commended, and their zeal is ever to be admired. The one problem for Protestants to solve is whether to accept Jesuitical, papal education, and thus become papal, forming "an image to the Beast,"—to use the language of the Apocalypse—or whether they will follow the principles of Christian education, and remain true to the name Protestant. Let the reader forget the names; but let him remember that there are but two *principles* in the world, when the standard of eternal truth is recognized; one exalts Christ, and gives life everlasting; the other exalts man, and its life is for this world alone.

Education according to the second does, in its methods, dwarf, enfeeble, and belittle. It puts stress upon the unimportant, and passes by truth without a glance. It prepares the mind for absolutism both in government and religion. Education according to the first will be based upon methods which develop, in every particular, the human being. It is a mental, moral, and physical education, and its object is so to educate that eventually each of these three natures will assume the right relation to the other two, and again, as on the Mount of Transfiguration with the Son of God, "divinity within will flash forth to meet divinity without."

Chapter XIV
America and the Educational Problem

PROTESTANTISM AND REPUBLICANISM, BORN OF THE REFORMATION, NOURISHED BY SCHOOLS.—As if lifted from the bosom of the deep by the mighty hand of God, America stood forth to receive the principles of religious and civil freedom born of the Reformation on German soil. To the German government was first offered the opportunity of developing to the full the reform movement. This full and complete development would have meant religious liberty for all, and a government by the people—Protestantism and republicanism. These two systems go hand in hand, and are more closely connected than any other principles in existence. The death of one means the death of the other, for the same lifeblood nourishes both.

Germany started well. There were to be found princes, liberal in mind and government, who accepted the new religion, and stood by the Reformers through all their storm-tossed career. God had raised up these men for the time and place, as surely as he called Nebuchadnezzar, or appointed a work for Cyrus. Protestantism was firmly rooted, and, as we have already seen, during the first forty years of its existence, so strong was its vitality that men and nations bowed before it. The early Reformers, especially Luther and Melanchthon, connected the movement with the fountain of life when they introduced a system of Christian education. And previous chapters make plain the truth that the life of the entire movement in its twofold aspect—Protestantism and republicanism—depended upon a right educational system. When the mass of German youth sat at the feet of

German teachers, and those teachers were true to the principles of Christian education, Roman influence dwindled, and her very life was threatened. It was then that the papacy itself took up the subject of education, and by the work of the Jesuits succeeded in killing the Reform in Germany—indeed, in all Europe.

"A day of great intellectual darkness has been shown to be favorable to the success of popery. It will yet be demonstrated that a day of great intellectual light is equally favorable for its success."

The Jesuits planted schools of their own in the shadow of Protestant schools; they entered Protestant schools as teachers; they sucked the life-blood from the young child, and it faded and died. The principles of the Reformation found honest hearts in the Netherlands. The Dutch took up the question of education; but the Jesuits were again on the track, and, as Ranke says, "They gradually carded their point." The Reformation crossed the Channel, to find the hearts of Englishmen longing for greater freedom. Lollardism, started by Wycliffe two hundred years earlier, sprang anew into life in the hearts of the Puritans, until, in the reign of Henry VIII, more than one half of the English population was Protestant. Finally, the Commonwealth was established.

To England was offered the opportunity of showing to the world the perfect fruits of the Reformation in its Protestant religion and a republican government. But alas! the story is repeated. English youth fell into the hands of Jesuits. An English college was founded at Rome, and teachers, ministers, and canvassers returned to their native land with the avowed purpose of their educators, the Jesuits, to overthrow the Reformation. And England fell!

Those familiar words from the pen of Luther, which appear in his letter appealing for aid in the establishment of Protestant schools, echo through England also: "The Word of God and His grace are like a shower that falls, and passes away. It was among the Jews; but it passed away, and now they have it no longer. Paul carried it to Greece; but in that country also it has passed away, and the Turk reigns there now. It came to Rome and the Latin empire; but there also it has passed away, and Rome now has the pope. O, Germans, do not expect to have this Word forever!" Could this man of God have come forth from his grave a century later, and have looked over his loved Germany, and over England, he would have added these names to those of the countries where God's Word and His grace had been, but had passed away. Must the name of America be added to the above list? May Protestants be aroused before it is too late!

Finding that England closed her doors against progress, the Puritans sought greater freedom in the Netherlands. They were disappointed, for they could not there educate their children as Protestantism taught them that they should be educated. As Pilgrims they sought new homes in America, finding a retreat on the bleak shores of New England. It is now our duty to trace the growth and decline of Protestantism in our own land. *Its prosperity in every other country has been in proportion to its adherence to the correct principles of education; its decline has without exception been the result of a wrong system of education.* How is it in the United States?

No student of history, and especially of prophetic history, doubts for a moment that the way was divinely prepared for Protestantism to cross the Atlantic, and it is equally as evident that that same Hand was upholding those principles after they reached these shores. God's Word spoke often to the hearts of men, leading them to devise plans, pass laws, establish institutions, and in various ways to so work that His truths might here grow to a perfection which they never reached in the old country. On the other hand, those teachings which have frustrated the principles of Protestantism in Europe are seen to be at work in America from the first planting of a colony until the present day. That strength-producing element was *Christian education*; that counteracting influence was *false* or *papal education*. These two elements form the subject of this chapter.

United States history is interwoven with the history of education. Her founders, especially of the New England colonies, traced their origin to an educational center in England, and as early New England history circles about Harvard, so the fathers and supporters of that institution traced their origin in Old England to the counties of East Anglia, where Cambridge University bore sway. "Of the first six hundred who landed in Massachusetts, one in thirty, it is said, was a graduate of the English Cambridge. These and their companions were rare men. They had the schooling for a service the like of whose execution, in completeness and good sense, the world has never equaled."[155]

"With matchless wisdom they joined liberty and learning in a perpetual and holy alliance, binding the latter to bless every child with instruction, which the former invests with the rights and duties of citizenship. They made education and sovereignty co-extensive, by making both universal."[156]

John Fiske enlarges upon this thought.[157] The "greater hospitality of Cambridge [University, England] toward new ideas" is proverbial, and the very names, Lincolnshire, Norfolk, Suffolk, and Essex, Cambridge and Huntingdon, familiar in the geography of New England, are telling a story of Protestant education.

Strong as the Puritans seemed in denouncing the Church of Rome, and in accepting Protestantism, which, at the beginning of the seventeenth century, more than ever before, meant separation from the established church and the established forms of government they, were not united in thought. There were two classes: Puritans, and a class of this class represented by such men as Richard Hooker. Of the Puritans, Fiske says: "Some would have stopped short with Presbyterianism, while others held that 'new presbyter was but old priest writ large,' and so pressed on to Independency."[158] This difference of opinion on religious matters is discernible when representatives of both classes, mingling in the society about Boston, started the educational work of America. Those inclined to remain under the banner of Presbyterianism taunted the others, who were known as Brownists, or Separatists, and who followed William Brewster to America, with *anarchy*, merely because they believed in carrying out fully the principles for which all were ready to fight.

Thus, from the first has our educational work fallen into the hands of two classes of men—a class willing to compromise in order to keep peace, and a bold, daring class, who advocated stepping out on truth regardless of what might follow.

There was a mighty educational problem before the church. The Episcopalians had failed to take up that work in England; it was from their midst that Wm. Brewster, a Cambridge graduate, John Robinson, who also was graduated from Cambridge in 1600, and William Bradford, afterward governor of Plymouth for thirty years, withdrew to form the nucleus of the Congregational Church, which had its origin at Scrooby, England, and ended in Plymouth. What Episcopalianism had overlooked in the matter of education in England it now became the duty and privilege of the new church to begin on the virgin soil of America.

The reader is familiar with the fact that the Puritans, leaving England because of civil and religious oppression, the result of a union of church and state, came to America for freedom, and, contrary to what one would expect, especially at a casual glance, they here developed a theocracy. "The aim of Winthrop and his friends in coming to Massachusetts was the construction of a theocratic state which should be to Christians... all that the theocracy of Moses and Joshua and Samuel had been to the Jews....In such a scheme there was no room for religious liberty....

The state they were to found was to consist of a united body of believers; citizenship itself was to be co-extensive with church membership."[159]

It is equally well known, however, that this theocratic form was soon broken; and while the United States is beginning to find herself again approaching this mode of government, it is a remarkable fact, and one well worthy of our closest consideration, that *the ancient theocracy of New England was broken by the power of the educational system* there introduced. When this is read from the pages that follow, let the reader answer the question whether or not the *repudiation of Protestant principles and the principles of republicanism by the United States in the nineteenth century is equally due to the present system.* Bear in mind the question as we proceed.

The educational history of the United States may conveniently be studied in three sections; 1. Colonial; 2. Revolutionary; 3. Nineteenth century.

I. The Colonial Period

Since Harvard College, the American Cambridge, "accomplished," as Boone says, "a much-needed work, with manifold wholesome reactions upon society and government, so that it has been affirmed, with show of truth, that 'the founding of Harvard College hastened the Revolution half a century,' "[160] our study of the schools of the colonial period will center around this institution. It can be stated with safety that the history of Harvard, its leading men, and its varying attitude toward different Colonial problems, throws light on the development of the question of education at the time when the foundations of our national government were laid.

When Boston was but six years old, plans were laid for America's first college. "Among the early educational leaders," says Boone, "were such men as the Rev. Thomas Shepherd, John Cotton, and John Wilson, Jr.; all clergymen and all college-bred; Stoughton; Dudley, the deputy-governor; and, above all, 'Winthrop, the governor, the guide and good genius of the colony.' Such were the men...of the infant colony....Here were learning and character; world-wisdom and refinements of heart; breadth and wholeness of culture, such as could alone justify the boldness of their attempt."[161] The institution was started in poverty; four hundred pounds being voted by the people. The high motive which prompted the enterprise was "an unbounded zeal for an education, that to them seemed not so much desirable as necessary, *that 'the light of learning might not go out, nor the study of God's Word perish.'*"

The object of the school, as held by the founders, is well described by a Boston citizen, who writes thus in 1643 to some of his friends: "After we had builded our houses, provided necessaries for our livelihood, reared convenient places for worship, and settled the civil government, one of the next things we longed for and looked after was to advance learning and to perpetuate it to posterity, dreading to leave an illiterate ministry to the churches, when our present ministers shall lie in the dust. And as we were thinking and consulting how to affect this great work, it pleased God to stir up the, heart of one Mr. Howard (a godly gentleman and a lover of learning, then living among us) to give the one half of his estate...toward the erecting of a college, and all his library."

In the contemplation of a college by those noble men, the uppermost thought was *how to gain an educated ministry*. This object was lost sight of.

"It must be remembered," writes Boone, "that for sixty years the institution was little more than a *training-school for ministers*, managed as a theological seminary, having religion, of a more or less well-defined type, as its basis and chief object. Yet, as Professor Emerson has put it, 'It is one of the most remarkable things in the history of Harvard, that, in all the constitutions of the college there is *nothing illiberal or sectarian; nothing to check the freest pursuit of truth in theological opinions, and in everything else;* and this, too, while the founders of the college were severely and strictly orthodox, often exclusive in their own opinions, and while their object was unquestionably to provide for the thorough education of ministers of the gospel in like views with themselves.' " "The very foundation idea of the college," says Boone, in another paragraph, "was the theological want."

"The presidents and members of the corporation were generally the prominent scholars, the theologians, and the political leaders of the community and time. The college easily came to be the arena upon which, or the interest about which, were fought those terrible logomachies of dogma and doctrine. These required, as they had, the best learning, the shrewdest insight, the most politic minds of the day."

This perhaps explains that former statement, that the education of ministers by Harvard had more than anything else to do with the overthrow of the theocracy established about Boston. It is interesting, also, to note the spirit of democracy which this institution fostered. In speaking of the raising of the fund for erecting the building, Boone says: "The colony caught his [Mr. Harvard's] spirit, and all did something, even the indigent. One subscribed a number of sheep; another, nine shillings' worth of cloth; one, a ten-shilling pewter flagon; others, a fruit-dish, a sugar-spoon, a silver-tipped jug, etc....No rank, no class of men, is unrepresented. The school was of the people."[162] "It was nursed by democracy," and it in turn nursed democracy. Surely the Spirit of God was pleading with men so to arrange their leading educational institution that the principles of the Reformation might be perpetuated.

The course of study for this ministers' school, as described by Emerson, was remarkably free from sectarianism, and liberal in thought. "The Bible was systematically studied for the entire three years, Ezra, Daniel, and the New Testament being specified. A year was given to catechetical divinity."[163] Students were required to attend worship twice daily, when the Scriptures were read in Hebrew or Greek, and they were required to translate the selection. History received some attention, but the sciences were practically unknown, and "all profane literature was excluded."

Through all this is discernible the attempt to educate for the cause of Christ. With this beginning, what might have been accomplished had the plan, with truth unadulterated, been followed! The work done in later days by the schools, Under the direction of the state, is but an indication of the broad field which lay ahead of Harvard and similar institutions, *had the church remained in her province as the educator of her own children.*

From the very foundation of Harvard may be seen indications that there was alongside of these principles of Christian education somewhat of medieval teaching, which, unless discovered and banished would act as leaven, permeating the whole loaf. For instance, when the college was less than twenty years old, we find this requirement for admission announced: "When any scholar is able to read Tully or any like classical Latin author, *ex tempore*, and make and speak true Latin in verse and prose, and define perfectly the paradigms of nouns and verbs in the Greek tongue, then may he be admitted to the College; nor shall any claim admission before such qualifications." Tiffs, of course, was patterning after the European universities, and theirs was a papal system.

This was the Harvard of colonial times. As we enter the Revolutionary period, we may look for changes as the result of both the correct and the incorrect principles harbored. Is Harvard, with all her wonderful facilities, training as many for gospel service today as she did of old? Yale, the second Congregational school, followed closely the plans and object of Harvard.

William and Mary, the second college in the United States, was founded under different circumstances. It was born in the midst of wealth, and was befriended by cavaliers and courtiers. "The roots," says Boone, "were deep in the great English ecclesiastical system," and yet the avowed object was "that the college, when established, should be a 'seminary for the breeding of good ministers.' " Notwithstanding good intentions, it mixed scholastic teachings; for, it stood for "the Oxford order of humanities; the *abstract* as the foundation of the concrete; everything for discipline; the ancient languages before the modern." Jefferson was a graduate of this school, and later it will be seen how this man, whose mind comprehended so clearly the principles of religious liberty, strove to break away from this mixture in education, and advocated a decidedly secular education in schools which were supported by the state, thereby avoiding in such institutions the mixture of secular and religious training.

So far, we see the Episcopal school, William and Mary, deeply rooted in the English ecclesiastical system, and unable to receive the Reformation principles of education pure and simple. The two Congregational schools, Harvard and Yale, approached more nearly the Protestant ideal, but being unable to break wholly the bond of scholasticism, they made much of preparatory work in the classics.

Some of the educational problems with which our Colonial fathers had to wrestle were "parental responsibility, the general viciousness of indolence, the educative office of labor, the state's relation to individual need, compulsory employment and schooling, the state ownership of child life," and above all, and including all, the relation the church sustained to the schools, how far secular education could be offered in Christian schools, and how far the church could ask aid of the state in the conduct of church schools. They were weighty questions upon which hung, and still hangs, the destiny of a nation.

No sharp dividing line can be drawn between the Colonial and the Revolutionary periods. The work begun in the Colonial period prepared men to act a noble part in the Revolutionary period. The *truth* of the educational system would bear fruit, but the error which we have already noticed, was in great danger of gaining strength enough to choke the pure principles. Mere accusations amount to but little. Let it suffice to follow the history of educational progress through the next century. Results speak for themselves.

II. The Revolutionary Period

In addition to the instruction given by pious Puritan parents to the flock in their own homes, a limited number of common or church schools was established in the Colonial period. The position of academies, as they develop in the Revolutionary period, is significant. We find that "alongside each of the first colleges, frequently antedating them, sometimes forming part of the organization, was a grammar-school."

Such schools, attached to Harvard, Yale, Princeton, William and Mary's, and others, prepared for the universities, and supplemented the work of the elementary or common schools. Herein lay a vital point. They had home schools, elementary schools, and colleges. It was impossible for these elementary schools to fit students for university life when such schools required for entrance that the student should "read Tully or any like classical Latin author *ex tempore*, and make and speak true Latin in verse and prose, and decline perfectly the paradigms of nouns and verbs in the Greek tongue," as has already been quoted from an early Harvard announcement. The universities founded by the church were, then, forming a course of study for these grammar schools, or academies, as they were soon called; and since the demand was for a classical preparatory school, naturally their courses were "fitted to the time-sanctioned curriculum of the college. They taught much Latin and Greek, an extended course in mathematics, and were strong generally on the side of the humanities." This was a modeling after Rugby, Eton, and other noted English schools, or the classical drill-schools of Germany, which, as we have before seen, were schools bearing decided marks of Jesuit teaching.

Should a young man care to pursue his studies beyond the elementary school, his only opportunity to do so was in one of the academies where the classics formed the sum and substance of the instruction. The tendency to revert to the established forms of European education, or the papal system, is plainly visible.

The first colleges had been planted to give a Christian training, and doubtless had a start which might have resulted in the greatest strength to the church, and to the nation in a secondary way; but the introduction of these grammar schools or academies, with a course of study in the *classics* made necessary by the universities, threw the majority of the young people into a *classical instead of a practical line of instruction*. Looking at it from one standpoint, no wiser move could have been made to turn the tide of educational reform again toward papal education. Can we here trace the footprints of the Jesuits, whose policy since the days of Loyola had been to overthrow Protestantism by a false system of education?

The effect of the mixture of the pure and the impure methods, traceable in indistinct lines at the very beginning, now assumed more definite proportions. The growth of academies was remarkably rapid, and when attention is called to such men as Franklin, the Adamses, John Hancock, and the generation of " '76," who received most of their education in these schools, it may seem like sheer presumption to condemn their work. The results, however, as seen in later years, warrant the charge that at that time was taken a long step from the principles of the

Reformation, which meant to this country a weakening both in Protestantism and republicanism.

These academies were denominational, it is true; still they offered this prescribed course of instruction. Almost immediately appear signs of the result of this union of Christian education with scholasticism. For instance, we read that "Brown University, though founded as a Baptist institution, was nevertheless one of the first schools of the period to emphasize the growing sentiment for a thoroughly undenominational collegiate training." Why should a denominational college give an undenominational course of instruction, and why, above all denominations, should the Baptists do so, to whom such a flood of light had come, and who always with pride pointed back to Roger Williams and the State of Rhode Island as the ancestors and embodiment of all that is Protestant and republican? But this is not the only indication of this decline from early principles.

About 1793 Harvard assumed the name of university. Boone says, "Signs of Catholicity also appear, in that students were no longer required to attend the divinity lectures, except they were preparing for the ministry....Literary societies, voluntary associations for social and general culture, were multiplied."

"The first Greek fraternity—the Phi Beta Kappa—the parent of both secret and open college fraternity organizations of America," was formed at William and Mary in 1776. This is another indication of the stealthy introduction of principles opposed to democracy, and which tend to break existing prejudice against the secret organizations of the papacy.

Again, "Yale, also, though nominally on a Congregational foundation, received aid (1792) from the state, and gave place in her corporation to state representatives." Educational apostasy was beginning; religious decline must follow.

Boone gives another paragraph, which, in a few words, tells a story of much significance, more, perhaps, than the author realized; for he was merely chronicling the history of education, not searching for the philosophy thereof. He says, "The college, once an appendage to the church, was seen, in view of imminent state dangers, to have an equal value to the Commonwealth." This, of course, is true, because the Commonwealth depended for support, for very existence, upon the educational ideas propagated in its schools. But the writer continues: "First encouraged because it provided an educated ministry, there was coming to be recognized an opinion, despite the deficiencies in culture, that education is something more—that it has a value in itself; that schools might well be maintained apart from the church as an organization, and in no way lessen their usefulness."[164] Here was the challenge.

God has placed in the hands of his church the right and privilege to educate the young. In doing this, he has done more; for in educating the youth, the church stands at God's right hand to guide the nation into paths of rectitude. Not by joining hands can this be done, for *church and state must, in order each to be free, be forever separate.* Still the pillar upon which the nation must stand, the only one upon which it *can* stand, is a *true system of education*, and this is a divine gift to the church, which was born of the Reformation.

To the Lutheran Church the message of education was preached by Luther. The Episcopal Church received this "word and grace of God," as Luther expresses it; but it passed from them, and they returned to scholasticism. Oxford, Cambridge, Eton, Rugby, all English schools testify to this. The message passed on to the Congregational Church, and Harvard, Yale, and others started on the right road, but through the glories of the world lost sight of their original object. Harvard, founded to educate ministers, sent forth in the year 1896, out of a class of four hundred graduates only six ministers." The Presbyterian Church had its opportunity, and likewise the Baptist and the Methodist. Rapidly education, the scepter with which America was to be ruled, was slipping from the churches. "Of the four colleges established during the war, two were non-sectarian, as were three fourths of the sixteen colleges founded in the twenty years after 1776."

A momentous time was reached. Not only were the colonies to organize government which would astonish the world, but the people of these colonies were on the verge of an educational precipice, and mighty interests were hanging in the balance.

We have seen that from the classical academies came forth the minds which, for a generation or two, bore sway while the nation passed its critical period. There were the Adamses and Jefferson, Franklin, Webster, De Witt Clinton, Horace Mann, Joseph Henry, Everett, and Story; Guilford, of Ohio; Grime, of South Carolina; Frelinghuysen, of New Jersey; Wayland, in Rhode Island; and Shaw, in Virginia; besides Kent, Clay, Marshall, and Randolph, who were, many of them, not only solving political problems, but exerting an influence in the school systems planned for their several states.

Many of these were classical academy men, and we can but see that the education received in these schools must affect the systems they would father in their several states. Had the colleges remained true to their trust with Christian education, the academies would have been preparatory schools for Christian colleges, and men sent forth from their walls would have been firmly grounded in the principles of Christian education, going forth into every state of the Union to found Christian schools which would in their turn make earnest and valiant youth, true to Protestantism and true to republicanism.

When the church fails to educate, men turn to the state. These men "differed in their views about the Constitution, and wrangled over the dangers of centralization; the best men were fearful of the inroads of slavery and the dangers to commerce," says Boone, "but all agreed that intelligence was necessary to citizenship." Washington said, "In proportion as the structure of a government gives force to public opinion, it is necessary that public opinion should be enlightened," and Jefferson urged that "the diffusion of light and education are the resources most to be relied on for ameliorating the condition, promoting the virtue, and advancing the happiness of man."

There is a demand for the highest and most practical kind of education. Statesmen see that statesmen, *citizens*, are needed. The denominational colleges ceased to educate Christians, and citizens must be educated elsewhere. In 1805 the Public School Society of New York City, was formed; the claims of public primary education were urged in Boston in 1818; and New York provided for the county supervision of schools. Early in the nineteenth century were either introduced or else discussed the first high schools, manual training schools, and mechanics' institutes, teachers' associations, teachers' publications, professional schools, and free public libraries.

We have entered the third period.

Chapter XV
America and the Educational Problem (Continued)

III. The Nineteenth Century

THE problem of elementary preparatory education fell from the hands of the churches, and was taken up by the state. What is the character of that education which the state can rightfully support? A momentous question indeed; but before considering it, let us investigate the schools that the state has organized, and which it did, and still does, support. There was an urgent demand for liberal education, and several states appropriated lands toward a school fund. As early as 1786 "New York State set apart two lots in each township of the unoccupied lands, for 'gospel and school purposes;' " and by a vote of about eighteen hundred, devoted the proceeds of half a million acres of vacant lands to the support of the common schools. Other states followed the same general plan, some in rapid succession, others more slowly. One thing was a settled fact—the education of the common people, passed over by the churches, had been taken up by the government.

Under those circumstances it is not surprising that in 1837, Horace Mann, president of the Massachusetts Senate, interested himself in the subject of education. Of this man it is said, "Rarely have great ability, unselfish devotion, and brilliant success been so united in the course of a single life." This man became the father of the public-school system of the United States, and began a work which long before should have been started by the popular churches of America. But it was neglected by them, and it will be profitable for us to watch the development of the grandest system of schools ever organized—a system which, if the subject of Christian education could be dropped, and it be viewed alone from the standpoint of the politician, has brought the United States into prominence as an educational center among the nations of the world. However, since *republicanism rests in the basin of Protestantism, and Protestantism is cradled in Christian education,* the moment the feature of Christian education is laid aside, and the system purports to be civil (but in fact it is never really that), that moment it loses its real vitality and genuine strength. But to return to Mr. Mann and his wonderful work.

Boone says: "The gnarls of a century's growth were to be smoothed; not all of the large number of private schools were in accord with the new movement, and the churches were naturally watchful of the encroachments of unsectarian education."[165] This expression describes the sectarian schools as in much the same attitude as that assumed by the weakening Christian church about the days of Constantine; and as the church of those days held out its hands to a stronger power for aid, and because it had lost its individual supply of strength—the Spirit of God—so now these sectarian schools watched with a jealous eye the progress of unsectarian schools, and, unable to hold their former and their allotted position by virtue of inherent strength, they reached out their hands to the state coffers, and received aid. Yale did it before the days of Horace Mann; many others have done it since.

Boone continues: "Incompetent teachers were fearful, politicians carped, and general conservatism hindered" by the advances of Mr. Mann. "Much was to be accomplished, also, within the school. Teachers had to be improved, interest awakened, methods rationalized, and the whole adjusted to the available resources. Moreover, school architecture had to be studied. All this Mr. Mann did." How great was the opportunity which the religious sects of America had missed! Some of the things which were accomplished in the next few years are thus reported: "A system of normal schools was originated. The annual appropriation for schools was doubled; two million dollars expended on houses and furniture;

the number of women teachers increased; institutes introduced and systematized; school libraries multiplied; education provided for the dependent, and young offending classes, and the first compulsory school law of the state enacted."

Henry Bernard, a young lawyer of Connecticut, did for
his state a work similar to that of Horace Mann in Massachusetts. He was a man of keen insight, and struck at the
root of many evils. Finding that public money was misap-
plied, and many primary children neglected, he went about
to work a reform. "Teachers were awakened, associations
for mutual improvement were formed....He established an
educational periodical," wholly at his own expense. In 1843
this strong-hearted, level-headed man was called by the state
of Rhode Island to straighten out the tangles in her educational system. From this beginning has grown the public
school system as seen today. It is interwoven in the meshes
of our national history from Boston to San Francisco, and
from St. Paul to New Orleans. The colleges had made necessary the academies—classical preparatory schools; and these
sent forth men who modeled the high schools after the aca-
demic course. The Christian colleges set the pace to begin
with; then, finding themselves outrun in the race, to meet the
needs, the nineteenth century sees a gradual but none the less
decided change in their courses of instruction. Here are a few
of the changes, with the reasons for them. Says Boone:—

"The current and recent magnifying of the humanities,
the growing recognition of an altruistic and co-operative
spirit in civil and social and political life, the increasing
complexity of social forces, new aspects of government,
the fundamental oneness of all life, and sequent idea of the
solidarity of human society, have created for the student
new lines of investigation."[166]

How true! How wide the separation between the ideal
held before the early Harvard and that of the Harvard of today. "The sequent idea of the solidarity of human society"
as a new line of investigation for students, seems almost
like mockery when we see the fundamental principles of

the government loosening, and ready to crumble on the application of some unexpected force.

The same departure from the study of God's Word and the record of his dealings with men and nations—God in history and politics—is noticeable in the curriculum of each modern college and university. To quote again from Boone, "The history of customs and institutions, the growth of opinions and sentiments as crystallized in social forms, the study of governments and religions, of art and industry, are clamoring for a place in the curriculum. Comparative philology, with the enlarged interest of modern languages, belongs to the present period." Such a curriculum cannot but have weight in molding the minds of men, and the history we are making today is but the resultant of the thoughts inculcated in our modern colleges.

The chair in science has been greatly enlarged: the ideas of evolution as advocated by Darwin, Huxley, and Dana have crept into the lecture courses, and having been received, bid fair to stay. Says Boone: "It has been said that biological study [in the universities] began with Huxley in England, and later in this country." "Of the several courses in Harvard, thirty per cent are in science, and in most other contemporary institutions a similar large ratio obtains. This has had its influence upon the accepted curriculum." This science would be termed by the Apostle Paul "science falsely so called."

"Great changes have occurred in the twenty years [since 1868] in the multiplication of courses and the accompanying specializations of study." Perhaps figures will be more impressive on this point than mere words. Boone states that "of the forty-seven higher institutions whose reports are given by Dr. Adams, including Harvard, Columbia, and Brown, and ten leading state universities, forty-six report an aggregate of *one hundred and eighty-nine* courses in history and closely related studies." Cornell now offers so many courses that should a student attempt to take them all, it would require more than the natural life of a man to complete them.

It is not with any spirit of condemnation that these things are stated, but it can be seen by all that there is a meaning which inevitably attaches to these changes. The multiplicity of subjects taught has led to a wonderful book study, and a student's whole life is spent in an attempt to put into his own head the thoughts which others have written for him. The spirit of the universities was caught by the academies, and by the high schools, and is reflected even in the lower grades. It is the beginning of the cramming process now so forcibly denounced by a few true educators. Readers of our magazines are familiar with the ideas expressed by Mrs. Lew Wallace in "The Murder of the Modern Innocents," by the editor of the *Ladies' Home Journal*, and others. I deem it sufficient to quote from Mr. Edward Bok, who startled American homes by stating that "in five cities of our country alone there were, during the last school term, over sixteen thousand children between the ages of eight and fourteen taken out of the public schools because their nervous systems were wrecked, and their minds were incapable of going on any farther in the infernal cramming system which exists today in our schools.... It was planned by nature that between the years of seven and fifteen the child should have rest—not rest which will stop all mental and physical growth, of course,...but the child's pace should be checked so as to allow him to recover from the strain which his system has just undergone.

"But what really happens to the child at the age of seven? Is he given this period of rest? Verily, no! He enters the schoolroom, and becomes a victim of long hours of confinement—the first mental application, mind you, that the child has ever known. The nervous wear and tear begins; the child is fairly launched upon his enjoyment (God save the mark!) of the great educational system of America....Special systems of 'marks,' which amount to prizes, are started, serving only to stimulate the preternaturally bright child, who needs relaxation most of all, and to discourage the child who happens to be below the average of intelligence. It is cramming, cramming, cramming! A certain amount of 'ground must be gone over,' as it is usually called. Whether the child is physically able to work the ground, does not enter into the question. And we do not stop even there! The poor children are compelled to carry home a pile of books to study, usually after supper, and just before going to bed, and that is about the most barbarous part of the whole system."[167]

This is enough to show that the system is recognized as practicing methods not in accordance with the laws of nature, which are the laws of God. Such methods are the result of the system at the head of which stand the colleges and universities which outline the work for all below them.

Parents read these statements with wonder and a feeling of horror, but only a few realize that the primary schools and the grammar schools, and even the high schools, are responsible for the health-destroying, brain-benumbing methods employed in our public schools. The cause for the present system and methods is to be searched for in the changes which time has wrought in those simple schools planted by the freedom-seeking Puritan fathers. Say, rather, that Protestantism offered a system of Christian education which, if it had been followed, would have prevented what we find today.

It is gratifying to find that the decline has not proceeded undisturbed. Its history has not sped on as a smooth-flowing river. From time to time men have arisen offering educational ideas in advance of the age in which they taught. Such men were Comenius and Pestalozzi, who introduced object-study in place of the time-honored memory work; and Froebel, whose patient labors for the children of the kindergarten have not only endeared him to the heart of the true teacher, but have made him a benefactor of mankind in that he aroused queries in regard to the methods of instructing the human mind. These men, searching for truths caught glimpses of the principles of true education as taught by Christ. Disciples of these men, instead of taking from them a borrowed light, have the privilege of going again to the source of true wisdom—"the Teacher come from God." Here is the secret of success for educational reformers of the twentieth century.

The tide has kept up a constant ebb and flow. When the tendency was growing strong toward the classics, natural science revived, and the spirit of investigation broke the band which memory work was weaving. Science, not content with lawful fields of exploration, is now delving into metaphysics, and sending to the world a race of skeptics and infidels; or, if professed Christians, students are confirmed evolutionists, casting aside the Word of God for the theories of geology, astronomy, or biology. The narrow cramming system of memory-teaching was killing the intellectual life of the children, when nature-study was introduced. This was an improvement indeed, for these studies are thought-producing; but here the tide set in the opposite direction, and faith in a Creator is destroyed.

As of Jerusalem, so now of the churches, they are destroyed because the education of the children is neglected. Wherein lies the safety of the Christian parent and his child? The child has a right to a Christian education. Where is it to be obtained? Can the state give it? It could not if it would. Are the Protestant churches educating their own children? Few indeed are the Christian schools, and today the churches are reaping the result of their long period of retrogression. The words of Dr. James M. Buckley, editor of the *Christian Advocate*, the leading organ of Methodism, voice the general sentiment. He says in part:—

"That the Methodist Episcopal Church, with nearly three million of communicants and a vast army of Sunday-school scholars, should add less than seven thousand to its membership in 1899, is startling. That in the same period it should show a decline of 28,595 in those avowed and accepted candidates known as probationers, is ominous. Such a situation has not been frequent in our history....No reverent person can charge the decline to God the Father Almighty, to Jesus Christ his only Son our Lord, or to the Holy Ghost, in whom the church ceaselessly declares its belief. It must therefore lie at the doors of every church."[168]

This statement is very true; and yet, while exonerating God, Christ, and the Holy Spirit from any blame in the matter, it is sad to note that prominent men in the ministry fail to see that the churches are losing their hold upon humanity because they have relinquished their right as Protestants to educate the children. The churches are to be pitied; but there is only one remedy, and that church which takes up its neglected duty in *education* will receive the reward. To the students of prophecy, it is a significant fact that this state of affairs has been growing deplorably worse since about the year 1843 or 1844.

The fluctuations which have occurred in the curricula of our leading schools has been referred to before, but is emphasized by a glance at the introduction of the elective courses. When the course of instruction became decidedly complex, requiring years for completion, and the multiplication of subjects made it impracticable for the majority of students to complete the course as outlined, there arose the privilege of option in the choice of the studies in many courses. This was also made necessary in the colleges by the organization of many technical schools throughout the land. "The early efforts to establish mechanics and manual-labor institutes are interesting as marking a reaction against the dominance of language and metaphysics, and an ingenious appeal for the large recognition of the physical sciences." This has led in some cases to the substitution of German or some other modern language, and an increased amount of mathematics in place of the classics, the students being free to choose.

This spirit of freedom, which has been almost wrenched, one might say, from many of the institutions of higher learning, is occasionally found to have swayed the hearts of earlier educators. One reads with keen relish the history of the founding of the University of Virginia, the moving spirit of which was Thomas Jefferson. The reader will be interested in a paragraph by Boone:—

"As early as 1779, while the 'Old Dominion,' with her sister states, was embroiled in a doubtful war; and again in 1814, after numerous defeats and constant opposition from the already-established William and Mary College, from the Protestant churches, and from most of the political leaders of the time, Mr. Jefferson and his friends sought to provide for the state, along with the general system of education, a university, in which should be taught in the highest degree, 'every branch of knowledge, whether calculated to enrich, stimulate, and adorn the understanding, or to be useful in the arts and practical business of life.' Five years later (1819) an act of the Assembly was obtained establishing the University of Virginia. When six years later it was opened, after a wide acquaintance and careful study of the most progressive institutions in the United States, it was found that in discipline and instruction, in constitution and means, it very materially differed from them all."[169]

The far-reaching sight of the chief promoter of the enterprise is seen when we note wherein lay this very material difference. "There is one practice," wrote Mr. Jefferson, "from which we shall certainly vary, although it has been copied by nearly every college and academy in the United States; that is, the holding of the students all to one prescribed course of reading, and disallowing exclusive application to those branches only which are to qualify them for the particular vocation to which they are destined. We shall, on the contrary, allow them uncontrolled choice in the lectures they shall choose to attend, and *require elementary* qualifications only, and sufficient age."[170]

This was a wonderful step for the time in which it occurred, and indicates the direction given to minds of men by the Spirit of God. The greater freedom occasioned by the adoption of the elective system is felt throughout the educational centers of our land. Johns Hopkins University grants the degree of B. A. in four out of six of its courses without the classics. This leads us, however, to a consideration of the question suggested several pages back, *What subjects can of right be taught in schools supported from the public funds?*

Education, pure and simple, in the breadth of its meaning, is character development. The state, as such, cannot judge of motives, hence it cannot educate the inner man. The two phases of the Reformation were Protestantism and republicanism; the first deals with the spiritual nature, and through this reaches the entire man, making a symmetrical character; the governmental part deals only with the mental and physical—

the outward manifestations. To the church was committed the charge of the spiritual man, and the commission to "teach all nations" given to the little company that watched the ascending Lord, was repeated to the church in the sixteenth century; and with especial weight was this burden laid upon the shoulders of American men and women. The state needs men to carry forward its pursuits; and for the purely secular training of such individuals, it has a perfect right, even a duty, to provide from the common fund. A purely mechanical, secular, or business course might therefore be offered in our state schools; but with such an education few parents are contented. The moral nature needs training; in order to be good citizens, it is argued, some part of the system of ethics which is based on the doctrines of Christ must be inculcated. Christian schools, and those only, can give a spiritual education. This is the dilemma in which the educational system found itself about the time of the Revolution, and the matter, instead of reaching a satisfactory solution, has grown steadily worse. The churches failed to provide for the Christian training; and the state felt that something must be done for the children. Public schools were established; but these, by right, cannot teach morality or anything pertaining thereto. But they do. Hence, the church by her failure has forced the state into the attempt to do her work—an impossible task.

Again, the churches and the denominational schools, not willing to be outdone by state institutions, have extended their stakes and lengthened their cords until they offer, not those subjects which are character building, so much as those which will enable them to compete with state institutions. Here again is a departure from Christian education, and a mixture which would be hard to designate as other than papal. Again, the state sets its seal upon work done in institutions which it supports, and the Christian schools—those in name at least—not only accept public money, but allow the state to put its seal to their work in the granting of literary degrees and diplomas. This is a natural result of the union of worldly education and the principles of Christian education which we have followed through two centuries, and yet today there is scarcely a school claiming to be Christian in its principles that dare raise its voice against the customs of its sister institutions.

"Render, therefore, unto Caesar the things that be Caesar's, and unto God the things which be God's," would be repeated, should the author of those words enter in person the institutions of learning which claim to bear his name. A union of church and state is described as the papacy; a union of education (the foundation of the church) and the state is passed by with scarcely a dissenting voice.

So far in this chapter, the educational work of the Catholic Church in the United States has been passed without a word—not because that organization has been less active here than in European countries, but because the idea is so prevalent that a system of education to be papal must emanate from the Roman Church. Ideas to the contrary have been emphasized again and again in these pages. In our own country we cannot fail to see that, aside from the work of the Catholic Church, there has been developed a papal system of instruction. The stepping-stones from the present back into the dim ages of the past, when Egypt or Greece swayed the world through science or philosophy, may in places be hidden; but the products of Greek philosophy and Egyptian wisdom, seasoned with the ideas of the medieval scholasticism, or the more subtle mixture of modern Christian education and the papal system as exemplified by Sturm, to which is attached the state's seal of approval, meet us from season to season as our schools send forth their graduates.

The Catholics, however, have not watched the growth of our educational system without putting forth a vigorous effort. From Colonial days, when the Jesuits flocked to these shores, and taught the established schools and missions, to the present, time, when the new university for the education of Catholic youth is in full operation at our national capital, this organization has spared no effort. As Boone says, "All other denominational service in education is partial and irregular compared with the comprehensive grasp of the Catholic Church. Their aim is all-inclusive, and assumes no other agency. Ignoring the public school, their plan is coextensive with their membership. With one fifth of all the theological seminaries, and one third of all their students; with one fourth of the colleges, nearly six hundred academies, and two thousand six hundred parochial schools (elementary), instructing more than half a million children, the church is seen to be a force which, educationally considered, is equaled by no other single agency but the government itself."[171]

The system by which this work is carried forward is thus described: "The twelve Catholic provinces... are subdivided into seventy-nine dioceses. The latter average from thirty-five to forty parishes, each of which is supposed to have a school for the elementary training of their children. As a matter of fact, *ninety-three per cent* of them maintain parochial schools, in which are educated, generally by the priesthood,...the 511,063 pupils. In addition to these are five hundred and eighty-eight academies, usually for the girls, and ninety-one colleges." This was written six or seven years ago, but the figures speak for themselves. With the nation honeycombed by schools which have as their avowed object the annihilation of Protestantism and republicanism; with our own public-school system, so grand in many respects, *yet compromising until it is indeed papal*, it is not strange that Methodist and Presbyterian congregations are bemoaning their dwindling numbers.

Should Protestants educate their own children? History speaks in emphatic language, Yes! The papacy says, If you wish us to have your children, No!

"God stands at the door and knocks; blessed are we if we open to him."— *Luther*.

Chapter XVI
Christian Education

AFTER watching the educational struggle which has gone on for ages between truth and error, and observing that scarcely a century has passed which has not witnessed a controversy more or less severe between Christian and papal methods of instruction, one is prepared to believe that this is a subject inseparably connected with the history of nations. This being true, we must expect to find ourselves in the midst of the controversy today. It needs but a casual glance at current history to confirm this fact; for minds are troubled because of existing evils, and hearts are open for educational truth.

If we are inclined to think that the principles of Christian education are new and before unheard of, we have but to catch the thoughts which have swayed true educators from the time of Christ to the present day to know that the same spirit has been at work in all ages to draw the hearts of men to God.

The advent of Christ was a wonderful event. "The Word was made flesh, and dwelt among us." That man might by Christ behold the workings of God in human flesh, and see here the manifestation of truth, Christ was born. His was pre-eminently a work of education, and His system was *Christian education*. By this means, heaven again reached earth, and clasped it to her bosom. Men, in their shortsightedness, were unable to comprehend the spiritual teachings of the Son of God, and often His most powerful lessons fell unappreciated on the ears of the multitudes, and even on the ears of the apostles.

Much as the life of Christ has done for the world there has never been a man or a nation of men, who have fully followed his teachings. Error has ever been mixed with truth, and the educators of the world have failed to see the realization of their hopes because of this partial grasp of truth.

Christ, when rejected by the world, did not withdraw entirely, and leave man to his fate; but He sent forth His Spirit, the *Spirit of Truth* as an educator, leading minds into truth. This working of the Spirit is plainly seen, for one man has been directed to one phase of true education, while another, perhaps a contemporary worker, or perhaps a successor, it may be a fellow countryman, or one at a great distance, has picked up another thread in the skein, and developed another thought for the world. The world has never long been left without some representative of Christian education. In attempting to define the term which stands as the subject of this chapter, attention is called to the partial work of reform which has been accomplished by men whom the world recognizes as educators. The errors of a false education, so prevalent in times past, and still recognized as a part of the educational systems now in vogue, stand in strong contrast to the correct ideas advocated by these men at various times.

The men whose ideas are given in this chapter lived and wrought after the Reformation; and in order to reveal the error against which they worked, it is necessary to consider the methods of instruction to be found in papal schools. Similar thoughts are found on previous pages, but, for the sake of contrast, they are here repeated.

Painter says: "When a young man had acquired a thorough mastery of the Latin language for all purposes; when he was well versed in the theological and philosophical opinions of his preceptors; when he was skillful in dispute, and could make a brilliant display from the resources of a well-stored memory, he had reached the highest points to which the Jesuits sought to lead him. *Originality and independence* of mind, *love of truth for its own sake, the power of reflecting, and of forming correct judgments, were not merely neglected,* they were suppressed in the Jesuits' system."[172] Karl Schmidt likewise testifies in the words, *"Books, words,* had been the subjects of instruction....*The knowledge of things was wanting.* Instead of things themselves, *words about the things were taught.*" "Learning by doing" is the rule in Christian education. A large amount of Latin and Greek was, and is still, the rule in the papal educational system, and these languages were taught, not for the sake of thought, but merely for the words. The world had for a century been bound by the study of the classics. This bondage was broken by the Reformation, but the world returned thither again. Milton, the poet of the seventeenth century, wrote: "Language is but the *instrument* conveying to us things useful to be known. Though a linguist should pride himself to have all the tongues that Babel cleft the world into, yet if he have not studied the solid things in them, as well as the words and lexicons, he were nothing so much to be esteemed a learned man as any yeoman or tradesman competently wise in his mother dialect only....We do amiss to spend seven or eight years in scraping together so much Latin and Greek as might be learned otherwise easily and delightfully in one year."[173]

Ratik, a German educator of the sixteenth century, said: "We are in bondage to Latin. The Greeks and Saracens would never have done so much for posterity if they had spent their youth in acquiring a foreign tongue. We must study our own language, and then the sciences." "Everything first in the mother tongue," and "nothing on mere authority," were rules in his schoolroom. Comenius, the renowned teacher, used to say: "If so much time is to be spent on the language alone, when, is the boy to know about things—when will he learn philosophy, when religion, and so forth? He will consume his life in preparing for life."

How exactly this applies to the word-study of our boys and girls today! It matters not whether it be Latin or English grammar; indeed, it may be that other mode of expression— some form of mathematics—where time and energy are devoted to the process merely. A failure to make the development of thought—independent thinking, in fact—the main object in instruction, stamps any method of teaching as papal, no matter by what name it is known, or by whom the subjects are taught. It was the life work of Comenius to counteract this tendency, as the following principles show. He insisted that "nothing should be taught that is not of solid utility." Nothing is to be learned by heart that is not first thoroughly understood." "Theologians and physicians should study Greek." "Doing can be learned only by doing." That educational reformers of today are advocating these same principles will be seen later. This is a part of Christian education.

John Locke, an English educator of the seventeenth century, had truth on the subject of education. Of the languages, he says: "When I consider what ado is made about a little Latin and Greek, how many years are spent in it, and what a noise and business it makes to no purpose, I can hardly forbear thinking that parents of children still live in fear of the schoolmaster's rod, which they look on as the only instrument of education; as if a language or two were its whole business."

Character was valued by this man, and his statement as to the relative importance of study is valuable to parents and teachers. "Reading and writing and learning I allow to be necessary, but yet not the chief business. I imagine you think him a very foolish fellow that should not value a virtuous or a wise man infinitely before a scholar. Not but that I think learning a great help to both, in well-disposed minds; but yet it must be confessed also that in others not so disposed, it helps them only to be the more foolish or worse men.

"I say this, that when you consider the breeding of your son, and are looking out for a schoolmaster, or a tutor, you would not have, as is usual, Latin and logic only in your thoughts. Learning must be had, but in the second place, as subservient only to greater qualities. Seek out somebody that may know how discreetly to frame his manners: place him in hands where you may, as much as possible, secure his innocence, cherish and nurse up the good, and gently correct and weed out any bad inclinations, and settle in him good habits. This is the main point; and this being provided for, learning may be had into the bargain."

To how great an extent are Protestants following this excellent advice? In what schools for Protestant boys and girls is innocence cherished? Where is the good nourished? Where are bad inclinations gently weeded out, and good habits settled? Where do these things take a position ahead of book learning?

"Virtue," continues Locke, "as the first and most necessary of those endowments that belong to a man or gentleman, was based on religion. As the foundation of this, there ought very early to be imprinted on his mind a true notion of God." Here one finds a clear conception of Christian education, which parents of today would do well to study.

The study of the classics, together with the memory work which was the chief characteristic of these studies, was not the only defect in papal education; hence it is not the only error from which educators, led, as one must believe, by the spirit of truth, have from time to time broken away. The cramming system, so justly denounced by thinking minds as one of the most far-reaching defects of the present school system, is a mark of papal education wherever it may be found. And probably no generation has passed which has not heard some voice lifted against this pernicious practice of the schoolroom. The God of heaven recognizes that the human mind contains the highest possibilities of earth; the child is a part of himself; and when wrong methods of education are used in dealing with developing minds, He, the head of the body, of which we are members, feels the hurt; so it is that Christian education is an emanation from the mind of God.

Montaigne, speaking of education in the sixteenth century, said: "It is the custom of school-masters to be eternally thundering in their pupils' ears, as if they were pouring into a funnel, while the pupils' business is only to repeat what their masters have said." He is taught that "a tutor should, according to the capacity he has to deal with, put it [the child's mind] to the test, permitting his pupil himself to taste and relish things, and of himself to choose and discern them....Too much learning stifles the soul, just as plants are stifled by too much moisture, and lamps by too much oil. Our pedants plunder knowledge from books, and carry it on the tips of their lips, just as birds carry seeds to feed their young....We toil and labor only to *stuff the memory*, but leave the *conscience and understanding unfurnished and void.*"

As late as January, 1900, Edward Bok, editor of the *Ladies' Home Journal*, wrote concerning the cramming process of the popular schools: "Do American men and women realize that in five cities of our country alone there were, during the last school term, *over sixteen thousand children* between the ages of eight and fourteen taken out of the public schools because their nervous systems were wrecked, and their minds were incapable of going on any further in the infernal cramming system which exists today in our schools?...Conservative medical men who have given their lives to the study of children place the number whose health is shattered by over study at more than 50,000 each year....It is cramming, cramming, cramming. A certain amount of 'ground must be gone over,' as it is usually called. Whether the child is physically able to work the 'ground' does not enter into the question."

The writer dwells upon the evils of night study, and continues: "True reform always begins at the root of all evils, and the root of the evil of home study lies in the cramming system."

Mrs. Lew Wallace says: "Go into any public school, and you will see girls pallid as day lilies and boys with flat chests and the waxen skin that has been named the school complexion. Every incentive and stimulus is held out; dread of blame, love of praise, prizes, medals, badges, the coveted flourish in the newspapers—the strain never slackens....The burden is *books*. The tasks imposed on the young are fearful. The effort seems to be to make text-books as difficult and complicated as possible instead of smoothing the hill so high and hard to climb.".

In her characteristic style, Mrs. Wallace condemns the usual methods of teaching arithmetic and language:—

"Said a mother, 'Two and two are what?' "

"The boy hesitated.

" 'Surely you know that two and two make four.'

" 'Yes, mama; but I am trying to remember the process.'

"Process, indeed!...

"One day Mary was bending over a tablet writing words on both sides of a straight line, like multiplied numerators and denominators.

" 'What are you at now?' asked grandma.

"Mary answered with pride, 'I am diagramming.'

" 'In the name of sense, what's diagramming?"

" 'It's mental discipline. Miss Cram says I have a fine mind that needs developing. Look here, grandma, now this is the correct placing of elements. *Fourscore* and *seven* are joined by the word *and*; a subordinate connective copulative conjunction. It modifies *years*, the attribute of the preposition. *Ago* is a modal verb of past time. The root of the first clause is—.

" 'Why, that's Lincoln's speech at Gettysburg. I keep it in my work-basket and know it by heart.'

" 'Indeed! Well, *ours* is a simple personal—.'

" 'That's enough. If President Lincoln had been brought up on such stuff, that speech would never have been written. He called a noun a noun, and was done with it.' "[174]

Montaigne could scarcely have given a more vivid description had he seen the grind of modern education, where grades are strictly kept, and all children, the strong and the tender alike, are forced through the same process. There is no relief save in dropping by the wayside when disease fastens its tendrils on the human frame.

Against this system all educational reformers have striven, but it remains with us still. Christian parents, could they see the relative value of soul and mental culture, would demand the establishment of a new order of things. Christian education alone can affect a cure.

Comenius strove to correct this error by the introduction of nature-study. He says: "The right instruction of youth does not consist in cramming them with a mass of words, phrases, sentences, and opinions collected from authors, but in unfolding the understanding, that many little streams may flow there as from a living fountain....Why shall we not, instead of dead books, open the living book of nature? Not the shadows of things, but the things themselves, which make an impression on the senses and the imagination, are to be brought before youth. By actual observation, not by a verbal description of things, must instruction begin....Men must be led as far as possible to draw their wisdom, not from books, but from a consideration of heaven and earth, oaks and beeches; that is, they must know and examine things themselves, and not simply be contented with the observations and testimony of others."

His fundamental principles were, "Education is a development of the whole man," and "Many studies are to be avoided as dissipating the mental strength."

A long stride was taken by Comenius toward breaking the mechanical teaching of the papacy. The error into which his followers fall is in making nature the all in all, failing to recognize the Word of God as the only guide and interpreter of natural phenomena. This mistake has led modern schools to take the position in science studies which is described in the following words by Frank S. Hoffman, professor of philosophy in one of America's leading theological schools: "Every man, because he is a man, is endowed with powers for forming judgments, and he is placed in this world to develop and apply those powers to all the objects with which he comes in contact."[175] In such words does he plainly state that human reason is the means by which man is to obtain his wisdom. Then follows his explanation of the method of procedure when reason has been thus exalted. These are his words: "In every sphere of investigation he [man] should *begin with doubt*, and the student will make the most rapid progress *who has acquired* the art of doubting well."

Suppose, now, that the subject under consideration is some newly discovered natural phenomenon, and the student of nature wishes to investigate. According to Professor Hoffman, a modern theologian, and hence a teacher, he must "begin with doubt, and the student will make the most rapid progress who has acquired the art of doubting well." Christian education, in contrast with this method, says, "Through faith we understand."

That this method of study—to begin with doubt—is not only applicable to the natural sciences, but to the study of spiritual truths also, Professor Hoffman continues: "We ask that every student of theology take up the subject precisely as he would any other science: *that he begin with doubt,* and carefully weigh the arguments for every doctrine, accepting or rejecting each assertion according as the balance of probabilities is for or against it....We believe that even the teachings of Jesus should be viewed from this standpoint—and should be accepted or rejected on the ground of their inherent reasonableness."

Thus, the spirit of doubt with which the child is taught to study nature, goes with him through all his school years; it grows with his growth; and if he enters a theological school to prepare for the ministry, he is confronted by the same method in the investigation of the teachings of Christ. What wonder that the results of modern education are a class of infidels and skeptics?

The words of President Harper, of Chicago University, are worth repeating: "It is difficult to prophesy what the results of our present method of educating the youth will be in fifty years. We are training the mind in the public schools, but the moral side in the child's nature is almost entirely neglected." Not only is it neglected, but faith is trampled to the ground, anal human reason exalted above its-prostrate form. *"When the Son of man cometh, shall he find faith on the earth?"* A pertinent question, indeed, for educators to answer.

This method of doubting is papal, and can be traced directly to Socrates, the Greek. Of him, we read: "Socrates was not a 'philosopher,' nor yet a 'teacher,' but rather an 'educator,' having for his function 'to rouse, persuade, and rebuke'....*Socrates' theory of education had far its basis a profound and consistent conception.*"[176]

In dealing with his students, the same authority thus states his method of procedure: "Taking his departure from some apparently remote principle or proposition to which the respondent yielded a ready assent, Socrates would draw from it an unexpected but undeniable consequence which was plainly inconsistent with the opinion impugned. In this way he brought his interlocutor to pass judgment upon himself, and reduced him to a state *of doubt* or perplexity. 'Before I ever met you,' says Meno, in a dialogue which Plato called by his name, 'I was told *that you spent your time in doubting, and leading others to doubt:* and it is a fact that your witcheries and spells have brought me to that condition; you are like the torpedo; as it benumbs anyone who approaches and touches it, so do you.' "

We can readily trace the connection between the Socratic method of doubting and the same method as advocated by the professor of the theological school, for "his (Socrates') practice led to the Platonic revival," and the Platonic system of education and its introduction in modern schools has been too thoroughly discussed in previous pages to need repetition here.

The Socratic method of teaching—the development of doubt—seems to characterize much of the teaching of to-day, if we can judge from an article which appeared in the *Outlook*, written by the editor, Lyman Abbott. The educational work is thus described:—

"The educational processes of our time—possibly of all time—are largely analytical and critical. They consist chiefly in analyzing the subjects brought to the student for examination, separating them into their constituent parts, considering how they have been put together, and sitting in judgment on the finished fabric of on the process by which it has been constructed.

"Thus, all or nearly all, study is analytical, critical—a process of inquiry and investigation. The process presupposes an inquiring if not a skeptical mood. *Doubt* is the pedagogue which leads the pupil to *knowledge*.

"Does he study the human body? Dissection and anatomy are the foundations of his study. Chemistry? The laboratory furnishes him the means of analysis and inquiry into physical substances. History? He questions the statements which have been unquestioned heretofore, ransacks libraries for authorities in ancient volumes and more ancient documents. Literature? The poem which he read only to enjoy he now subjects to the scalpel, inquires whether it really is beautiful, why it is beautiful, how its meter should be classified, how its figures have been constructed. Philosophy? He subjects his own consciousness to a process of vivisection in an endeavor to ascertain the physiology and anatomy of the human spirit; brings his soul into the laboratory that he may learn its chemical constituents.

"Meanwhile the constructive and synthetic process is relegated to a second place, or lost sight of altogether. Does he study medicine? He gives more attention to diagnosis than to therapeutics; to the analysis of disease than to the problem how to overcome it. Law? He spends more time in analyzing cases than in developing power to grasp great principles and apply them in the administration of justice to varying conditions. The classics? It is strange if he has not at graduation spent more weeks in the syntax and grammar of the language than he has spent hours in acquiring and appreciating the thought and the spirit of the great classic authors. It has been well and truly said of the modern student that he does not study grammar to understand Homer, he reads Homer to get the Greek grammar. His historical study has given him dates, events, a mental historical chart; perhaps, too, it has given him a scholar's power to discriminate between the true and the false, the historical and the mythical in ancient legends: but not to many has it given an understanding of the significance of events, a comprehension of, or even new light upon, the real meaning of the life of man on the earth. Has he been studying philosophy? Happy he is if, as a result of his analysis of self-consciousness, he has not become morbid respecting his own inner life, or cynically skeptical concerning the inner life of others.

"It is doubtless in the realm of ethics and religion that the disastrous results of a too exclusive analytical process and a too exclusive critical spirit are seen. Carrying the same spirit, applying the same methods, to the investigation of religion, the Bible becomes to him simply a collection of ancient literature, whose sources, structure, and forms he studies, whose spirit, he, at least for the time, forgets; worship is a ritual whose origin, rise, and development he investigates; whose *real significance* as an expression of penitence, gratitude, and consecration he loses sight of altogether. *Faith* is a series of tenets whose biological development he traces; or a form of consciousness whose relation to brain action he inquires into; or whose growth by evolutionary processes out of earlier states he endeavors to retrace.

"Vivisection is almost sure sooner or later to become a post-mortem; and the subject of it, whether it be a flower, a body, an author, or an experience, generally dies under the scalpel. It is for this reason that so many students in school, academy, and college lose not merely their theology, which is perhaps no great loss, but their religion, which is an irreparable loss, while they are acquiring an education."[177]

This spirit of doubt characterizes the teachings of higher critics. The critical study of the Bible, Dr. Newton tells us, "has disposed forever of the claim that it is such an oracle of God as we can submit our intellects to unquestioningly." "Dr. Briggs says that there are three co-ordinate authorities—the church, the Bible, and reason. 'But when they disagree, which is to be the final court of appeal?' asks Dr. Newton. 'They do disagree widely today.' Dr. Newton believes that the ultimate court of appeal is reason—not the reason of Thomas Paine and the present-day realistic rationalists, but rather the *'Divine Reason' of Socrates and of Plato*....Reason in this sense means not merely or chiefly the rationalizing faculty, but the moral nature—the whole spiritual being of man. It is what conscience teaches, as well as what intellect affirms, that, together with the voice of the heart, forms the trinity of true authority—of reason.' "[178]

This is indeed the exaltation of reason. There is, in such a system, no room whatever for faith. W. T. Harris, United States Commissioner of Education, writing of Sunday-schools, attributes their decline to the adoption, by Sunday-school teachers, of the methods employed in the secular schools. A few words from him will suffice. He says: "With the spectacle of the systematic organization of the secular schools and the improvement of methods of teaching before them, the leaders in the church have endeavored to perfect the methods of the religious instruction of youth. They have met the following dangers which lay in their path; namely, first, the danger of adopting methods of instruction in religion which were fit and proper only for secular instruction; second, the selection of religious matter for the course of study which did not lead in a most direct manner toward vital religion, although it would readily take on a pedagogic form."[179]

In order to show the reason why methods which are perfectly proper in giving secular education are not adapted to religious instruction, Mr. Harris explains: "The secular school gives positive instruction. It teaches mathematics, natural science, history, and language. Knowledge of the facts can be precise and accurate, and a similar knowledge of the principles can be arrived at. The self-activity of the pupil is... demanded by the teacher of the secular school. The pupil must not take things on authority, but must test and verify....He must trace out the mathematical demonstrations....He must learn the method of investigating facts.... The spirit of the secular school therefore comes to be an enlightening one, although not of the highest order."

The whole tendency of secular education, according to Mr. Harris, is to develop a spirit of investigation and proof. This, he says, is a means of enlightening, but not of the highest order. The highest means of enlightening the mind is by faith. That is God's method. Christian schools must avoid the secular methods of instruction, adopting in their stead that highest form of enlightening—faith. That separates Christian schools from secular schools in methods as well as in the subject matter taught.

This secular method of investigation saps the spiritual life, and is responsible for the decline in modern Protestantism. Mr. Harris continues: "Religious education, it is obvious in giving the highest results of thought and life to the young, must cling to the form of authority, and not attempt to borrow the methods of mathematics, science, and history from the secular school. Such borrowing will result only in giving the young people an over weening confidence in the finality of their own immature judgments. They will become conceited and shallow-minded....Against this danger of sapping or undermining all authority in religion by the introduction of the methods of the secular school which lay stress on the self-activity of the child, the Sunday-school has not been sufficiently protected in the more recent years of its history."

If the adoption of secular methods of teaching in the Sunday-school, where children are instructed one day only in the week, has so weakened Protestantism, what must be the result when children are daily taught in the public schools by methods which tend always to exalt human reason above faith. It is little wonder that five days' instruction cannot be counteracted by the very best Sabbath instruction even in those schools which have not adopted secular methods in teaching the Bible.

Protestants should learn from this that in starting Christian schools the methods followed in the secular schools cannot be adopted. Here is the stumbling-block over which many are apt to fall. Religious instruction demands methods of teaching which will develop faith.

I cannot refrain from recurring to the teachings of Comenius, since they so strongly opposed the methods of education followed by those who, today, claim to be his disciples. James H. Blodgett says: "Comenius, anticipating more modern leaders in the philosophy and the art of education, prepared an outline of the Pansophic School about 1650, in which the work of a complete education was divided for seven classes. The general school was to spend the first hour of the morning in hymns, Bible reading, and prayers."[180] "Class III, the Atrial" we are told by the same writer, "was to have the inscription, 'Let no one enter who cannot speak.' In this class the boys should begin to read the Bible....The history of this class is the famous deeds of the Biblical narrative." Of Class IV We read: "A special collection of hymns and psalms must be arranged for this class; also, an epitome of the New Testament, which should comprise a continuous life of Christ and His apostles, compiled from the four Gospels....The accessory study is Greek....It is comparatively easy to learn to read the New Testament [in Greek], and this is the chief utility of the study." Bible study formed an important feature of the work of Class V, for concerning its work we read: "A Bible Manual, also, called the Gate of the Sanctuary, is to be placed in the pupils' hands. This is to contain the whole of Scripture history in the words of the Bible, but so digested that it may be read in one year."

Class VII was theological; and the reader will readily note the difference between the course of instruction marked out for it by Comenius, and that suggested by Professor Hoffman for theological students in the twentieth century. "Inscription over the door: 'Let no one enter who is irreligious.'...The class book should be a work dealing with the last stage of wisdom on earth, that is to say, the communion of souls with God. Universal history should be studied, and in particular the history of the church for whose sake the world exists....The future minister must learn how to address a congregation, and should be taught the laws of sacred oratory."

Let it be remembered that Comenius was a bishop of the Moravian Brethren, a denomination noted for its extensive missionary work, its missions dotting the earth. Their activity in church work can readily be accounted for by their system of education. Any Protestant church which wishes to survive, and desires the spread of its principles, must see that its children are educated spiritually as well as mentally and physically.

We are now brought to consider another very important phase of education—the relation of mental to physical training. False systems have ever exalted the former to the neglect of the latter. Christ combined the two, and educators from the seventeenth century on have presented correct views on the subject.

Locke begins his "Thoughts on Education" with these words: "A sound mind in a sound body is a short but full

description of a happy state in this world." "The attainment
of this happy condition," observes Painter, "is the end of
education....In his [Locke's] mind, the function of education was to form noble men well equipped for the duties of
practical life."[181]

A pure soul in a sound body should precede study of
mere facts. Locke's ideas of education are thus described
by Quick: "His aim was to give a boy a robust mind in a robust body. His body was to endure hardness, his reason was
to teach him self-denial. But this result was to be brought
about by leading, not driving him. He was to be trained,
not for the university, but for the world. Good principles,
good manners, and discretion were to be cared for first of
all; intelligence and intellectual activity next; and actual
knowledge last of all....The prevalent drill in the grammar
of the classical languages was to be abandoned, and the
mother-tongue was to be carefully studied....In everything,
the part the pupil was to play in life was steadily to be kept
in view."

And yet today, when the editor of one of our magazines
proposed that our university students discuss the question,
"What order of studies is best suited to fit the average man
for his duties in the world of today?" or, "What is the relative importance of the various branches of education in
fitting a man to secure his own happiness and rendering
him a useful citizen and neighbor?" the president of Yale
University replied: "Some of the men hesitate to give the
official sanction of the university to a debate on short notice on questions of which most of the contestants know
very little. Why should not our university students know
and choose the practical studies? If they do not know them,
why not?"[182]

There are educators, however, who are willing to break
away from the conservatism of the past, and who advocate a change of methods in the elementary schools. Such
are the thoughts presented by the superintendent of public instruction in the State of Michigan, in a manual issued

in May 1900. There is sound sense in the following paragraphs, which will appeal to all who consider the needs of a child's mind. He says:—

"It is the duty of the schools to produce parallel growths of all the faculties, leaving the pupil free to swing out into the realm of choice with no distorted tastes or shortened powers. The training of the hand ministers to this parallel development.

"We remember when the sciences were taught wholly from the text. Later, the principles of Pestalozzi entered the class room, and we stood open-eyed and open-minded, as the truths of science were demonstrated with the proper apparatus in the hands of the teacher, but today Forebear's idea has taken possession, and the pupil performs the experiment. It is his hand that creates the conditions; it is his eye that watches the changes, his hand that notes them. Science teaching has thus adopted the manual training idea; and such are the results that Latin, Greek, and mathematics are no longer considered as the only intellective subjects for college training.

"What the manual training idea has done for science teaching: it will do for mathematics and other kindred subjects. The dissatisfaction among professional and business men regarding the teaching of practical things in our schools is widespread. This is especially true regarding arithmetic, penmanship, spelling, and language. Anyone who doubts this needs but to enter the business places of his own city and make inquiry. There is a well-grounded feeling that in the mastery of arithmetic is a discipline closely allied to that needed in the activities of life; and when a father discovers that his child of sixteen or seventeen years has no idea of practical business questions and little skill in analytical processes, he justly charges the school with inefficiency. The difficulty, however, is that the pupil has had no opportunity to sense arithmetic. To him measurements and values are indefinite ideas. He commits facts to memory, and blindly tries to work out problems. If his memory and imagination are good, he stands well, and receives a high mark. But still the work is vague; it does not touch his life or experience; it has no meaning. Put that pupil into a manual-training school—the boy in the shop, the girl in the kitchen [practical experience has demonstrated that the girl has a place in the shop also]—and at once mathematical facts become distinct ideas.

"Step into the shop of a manual-training school [or step into the well-ordered kitchen], and observe the boy with a project before him. What are the steps through which his mind must bring him to the final perfection of the work.

"First, he must give the project careful study.

"Second, he must design it and make a drawing of it. This at once puts mathematics into his hand as well as his head. He must use square, compass, try-square, and pencil. Exact measurements must be made, divisions and subdivisions calculated, lines carefully drawn.

"Third, he must select material of proper dimensions and fiber, and then must reflect how to apply it to the draught made so that there is no waste.

"Fourth, he must plane and saw to the line, correct and fit; in short, must create the project that has had existence in his mind and upon paper only. Then it is that his arithmetic begins to throb with life, his judgment to command, and his ethical sense to unfold."

This is the testimony of teachers who have made a practical application of arithmetic and geometry in the carpenter shop. Children twelve and fourteen years of age solve problems in proportion, in square root, in measurements, and in denominate numbers, which baffle the skill of the ordinary high- school graduate. This, too, is a part of Christian education. Doubtless Christ himself gained most of his mathematical knowledge at the carpenter's bench.

"The most practical education," says Hiram Corson "(but this, so-considered, pre-eminently practical age does not seem to know it), is the education of the spiritual man; for it is this, and not the education of the intellectual man, which is, must be (or Christianity has made a great mistake), the basis of individual character, and to individual character...humanity owes its sustainment." The proper combination, then, of religious training and practical hand work in teaching mathematics or language will develop stability of character, and this is the end and aim of Christian education.

There are, however, in this twentieth century, various other ways of rendering education practical; and since these ways are a factor in the Christian training of youth, they should receive attention. God made no mistake when he gave to Adam the work of tilling the soil. Since the days of Eden, those men who have shunned the cities, and chosen instead to dwell in rural districts, have, as a rule, come closest to the heart of the Creator. The true way to study the sciences is to come in touch with nature.

For this, also, we have the example of Christ. "In training His disciples, Jesus chose to withdraw from the confusion of the city, to the quiet of the fields and hills, as more in harmony with the lessons of self-abnegation He desired to teach them. And during His ministry He loved to gather the people about Him under the blue heavens, on some grassy hillside, or on the beach beside the lake. Here, surrounded by the works of His own creation, He could turn the thoughts of His hearers from the artificial to the natural. In the growth and development of nature were revealed the principles of His kingdom. As men should lift up their eyes to the hills of God, and behold the wonderful works of His hands, they could learn the precious lessons of divine truth. Christ's teaching would be repeated to them in the things of nature....The things of nature take up the parables of our Lord, and repeat His counsels."

The teacher who has a desire to ennoble the character of his pupils will seek a place where nature, in her silent language, gives lessons which no human tongue can utter. Parents who desire the best good of their sons and daughters, will, when the light of Christian education dawns upon their minds, hasten into the country, that the youthful minds over which they are keeping guard may be influenced by the natural rather than by the artificial.

It is not surprising that the best educators who have opened their minds to truth have taught that cultivation of the soil, with the training of the eye and the hand in the shop, should accompany mental discipline. Prof. James R. Buchanan says, "Blessed is the *farmer's boy*....The industrial feature, not limited to handicraft, but embracing all forms of useful exertion, *is the essential basis of a true education;* as it insures, if rightly conducted, a worthy character, a healthy constitution, a solid intellect, and a capacity for practical success; for it gives vigor to the entire brain, and a far better invigorating mental discipline than can ever be obtained from text-books. The boy who has constructed a wagon, or a bureau, or *raised a small crop*, as instructed, has more independence of mind and originality than the one who has only studied text-books. The boys of Lancaster, Ohio, who gave half their time to useful industry, made better progress in school studies than the common school pupils who had their whole time for study, and at the same time presented a model of conduct in all respects unequaled in any non-working school in this country."[183]

Close adherence to the text-book is the papal-method of teaching, and is a necessary accompaniment of prescribed courses, while the humanistic tendency is well developed. Christian schools, because of the truths they advocate, are forced to depart from the established order in the educational world, and their education is rendered practical by joining *the farm and the school*.

This method of teaching is already followed in some places, showing that that system so often designated Christian education is not a thing of recent birth, neither is it the product of some man's mind. Its principles have been made known from time to time, and these principles have been followed more or less carefully in all periods of the world's history.

That the combining of soil-cultivation and study is a practical thing, and not a mere theory, is attested by the words of United States Consul-General John Karel, who reports as follows concerning "School Gardens in Russia": "In a good many countries of western Europe, especially in Germany, Austria, France, Belgium, Switzerland, and partly in Sweden, the public village schools have sections of land allotted to them, which are either devoted to the use of the teachers, who take the profits there from, or serve for the establishment of school gardens. School gardens in western Europe bear, in a certain measure, a scientific character. Children are made to carry out in them practically what they learn theoretically.

"In Russia… it was well known that the land owners and peasants were in great need of instruction in farming; consequently, schools of all kinds were established by the ministry of agriculture throughout the country....For the development of the gardening industry, schools were founded first in Penza, in Bessarabia,… and in 1869 a school of gardening and viticulture was found at Nikitsk. The work of the Nikitsk school was divided as follows: During the winter semester there were three hours of lessons per day and four and one-half hours of practical study in the garden, vineyard, and in the cellar. During the summer semester the lessons in class lasted only one hour, or sometimes two hours, but the practical studies occupied daily six or even eight hours."[184]

Teachers in these schools are enabled to support themselves a least partially from the sale of fruits, berries, vegetables, honey, etc., but this was not the chief inducement in starting school gardens. The writer last quoted continues: "The desire to add something to the low salaries of the village school teachers, and, on the other hand, to acquaint as much as possible, not only children, but also grown-up people, with gardening, sericulture, and apiculture, has caused an increase during the last ten years, in the number of school gardens, apiaries, and silkworm hatcheries.

In 1892 there were about two thousand school gardens in Russia. At the present time [1897] there are 7,521, with 532 apiaries, and 372 silkworm hatcheries."

Mr. Mescherski, who is chief of one of the departments of agriculture, and one of the principal advocates of school gardens in Russia, has stated the object of school gardens and their significance as follows: "School gardens... are of importance on the following grounds. (1) Hygienic, as being a place for physical labor in the open air, so necessary for the teacher and pupils....(2) Scientific educational, as acquainting children with the life of useful plants, developing their minds by the study of nature, and promoting in the rising generation a regard for labor and a more moral and aesthetic sentiment concerning trees. (3) General economical... and (4) Personal economical," which refers to the support of the teacher.

If the Russian government, on the liberation of its serfs and its crown peasants, found it so greatly to its advantage to establish school gardens, of what lasting benefit would they be to Christians! Protestants, instead of crowding into the cities where the laboring man is subject to the trades unions, trusts, and monopolies, should seek for themselves a few acres of land, and should see that schools are established for the education of their children where the mechanical text-book grind is replaced by the study of God's will as revealed in His Word and works. Nature studies thus conducted, instead of developing doubt, will strengthen the faith of the pupil, and the students from such schools will be fitted for citizenship not only in the governments of earth but in the Kingdom of God. This also is a part of the system of instruction known as Christian education.

Chapter XVII
Christian Education (Continued)

THE nineteenth century has not been lacking in minds which have grasped at least in part, the principles of Christian education. Thus, writes Pestalozzi: "Sound education stands before me symbolized by a tree planted near fertilizing waters....In the new-born child are hidden those faculties which are to unfold during life. The individual and separate organs of his being form themselves gradually into an harmonic whole, and build up humanity in the image of God."[185]

With this agrees Milton's definition of education. "The end, then, of learning," he says, "is to repair the ruins of our first parents by regaining to know God aright, and out of that knowledge to love Him, to imitate Him, to be like Him, as we may the nearest by possessing our souls of true virtue, *which being united to the heavenly grace of faith,* makes up the highest perfection." This is similar to the definition given by the author of "Christian Education," that "the true object of education is to restore the image of God in the soul."

Christian education, then, is a spiritual education. In this sense the words of Pestalozzi, at the burial of his wife, are pathetic but weighty with significance. Turning to the coffin, he said tenderly· "We were shunned and despised by all; sickness and poverty bowed us down; and we ate dry bread with tears. What was it in those days of severe trial gave you and me strength to persevere and not lose hope?" Laying a copy of God's Word on her breast, he continued: "From this source you and I drew courage and strength and peace."[186]

Advocates of Christian education may today encounter the same sort of rebuff from the world; but God's Word stands as guide, expressing the principles to be followed by the educator.

Charles W. Dabney, Jr., president of the University of Tennessee, in an address gave utterance to these words. "The Bible is the best text-book of education, as of many other sciences. In it we read where Paul tells Timothy, his 'dearly beloved son in the faith,' that 'all Scripture is given by inspiration of God, and is profitable for doctrine, for reproof, for correction, for instruction in righteousness that the man of God may be perfect, thoroughly furnished unto all good works.' Nowhere in literature or philosophy is there a better or clearer expression of the true purpose of education than this. The object of education is not pleasure, or comfort, or gain, though all these may and should result from it. The one true purpose in education is to prepare the man for 'good works.' It is a noble thing to develop a perfect soul, to thoroughly furnish a body, mind, and heart.... Character building, conscience forming, then, is the main object of education. The teacher dare not neglect character, nor the college to provide for its development. We must always and everywhere, in every course and scheme of study, provide those methods and agencies which shall develop the character of the pupil along with his other powers. How, then, shall we develop character in our pupils? What are the methods and the agencies for doing this? This is the crucial question of this age, as of every age. To this question all the ages give but one answer, and that is Christianity. The world has had many teachers of science, art, and philosophy, but only one teacher of righteousness, and He was Jesus Christ, the Son of God."

The many teachers of science, art, and philosophy, have, by their systems of education, led men away from the knowledge of God, the wisdom which is eternal life. If the education of Christ is to be accepted, as suggested by Professor Dabney, His word, the Bible, must be recognized as the Book of books, the guide in all investigation, the interpreter of all phenomena.

Much is said concerning the moral education which every child should receive. Parents realize that the boy or girl who grows to maturity with only a physical or intellectual education is either a pugilist or a fit subject for the penitentiary, and hence they insist that the spiritual nature should receive some attention. But where is this spiritual education to be obtained? State schools have no right to give such training; indeed, they cannot do it. True, they have attempted it, but it is a miserable failure. Protestants should no longer make the demand. The time has come for them to see that they should establish schools, whose object it is to develop character. These schools should receive support independent of the state; they should be free to follow methods entirely different from the formalism of the papal system; their course of instruction should meet the individual needs of the pupils, and be of a character which will develop Christians. To accomplish such results, the Word of God must be taken from the dust, and placed in the curriculum, not as a mere reference book of Jewish antiquities, but, as it is in deed and in truth, the light whose rays encircle the world. "The Holy Scriptures must be the Alpha and Omega of Christian schools," wrote Comenius. Christ must be the teacher.

The men thus far quoted have followed the light which shone upon their pathway. Today we may gather the scattered gems of truth left by them; but, better far, we may go direct to the Word itself, and the Spirit of truth will guide into the paths of Christian education. As taught by Froebel, "The spiritual and physical development do not go on separately in childhood, but the two are closely bound up with each other."

The human being has a threefold nature—the physical, the mental, and the spiritual; and Christian education so develops these that they sustain the proper relation one to another. The spiritual nature was the controlling power in the man made in God's image. In the degeneration of the race, he lost his spiritual insight, and passed first to the intellectual plane, then to the physical. This is seen in the history before the flood. Eden life was a spiritual existence; Adam's life after the fall was less spiritual, and gradually his descendants came to live on the mental plane. There were master minds in the antediluvian world. Men had no need of books, so strong was the memory and so keen the insight. Through further disobedience, through an education which strengthened reason rather than faith, men sank to the physical plane instead of rising to the spiritual, until in due time the earth was destroyed by water.

The same planes of existence are distinguishable in all ages since the flood, but Christ alone rose to the purely spiritual level. Israel as a nation might have so lived had true educational methods been followed. Israel falling, the offer was made to the Christian church. Age by age that body has refused to live a spiritual life, or, accepting the proffered gift, has attempted to rise without complying with the necessary conditions—absolute faith in God's Word and strict compliance with His commands. The Reformation again turned men's eyes toward a spiritual education, and American Protestants had the best opportunity ever offered man to return to the original design of the Creator. Failure is again the verdict of the recording angel. Time hastens on, and the last gospel message is going to the world; but before *a people can be prepared for the setting up of Christ's kingdom, they must be educated according to the principles of Christian education,* for this is *the foundation* of all government as well as of all religion.

What is Christian education? Since its object is the training of a human being for life eternal, and that existence is a spiritual life, the spiritual must be the predominating feature of the education. When the spiritual leads, the intellectual and physical take their proper positions. The inner or spiritual man feeds only upon truth, absolute truth; not theory nor speculation, but truth. "Thy word is truth." *The Word of God must then be the basis* of all Christian education, the science of salvation the central theme.

Since God reveals His character in two ways, in His Word and in His works, the Bible must be the first book in Christian education, and the book of nature next. Many educators have seen the value of the book of nature, and today nature-study forms a large part of the course of instruction in all grades of schools. It may be asked, Is not this, then, Christian education? We reply, Does it restore in men the image of God? If so, it passes the test. But it cannot be said to do this, and therefore it falls short. Wherein, then, lies the difficulty in modern nature-teaching, or the sciences in general? Read some of our modern text-books in science. They readily reveal the answer.

Young's General Astronomy reads: "Section 908. Origin of the Nebular Hypothesis—Now this [the present condition] is evidently a good arrangement for a planetary system, and therefore *some have inferred* that the Deity made it so, *perfect from the first.* But to one who considers the way in which other perfect works of nature usually come to perfection—their processes of growth and development—*this explanation seems improbable, it appears far more likely that the planetary system grew than that it was built outright.*...In its main idea that the solar system once existed as a nebulous mass, and has reached its present state as the result of a series of purely physical processes, it seems certain to prove correct, and *it forms the foundation of all the current speculations upon the subject.*

"Section 909. La Place's Theory—(a) He supposed that at some past time, which may be taken as a starting point of our system's history,… the matter collected in the sun and planets was in the form of a nebula. (b) This nebula was a cloud of intensely heated gas, perhaps hotter, *as he supposed*, than the sun is now. (c) This nebula, *under the action of its own gravitation,* assumed an approximately globular form, with a rotation around its axis," etc., etc.

The student must decide whether he will base his study of the heavens and the earth—the study of astronomy, geography, arid geology, as well as zoology, and botany indirectly—on this hypothesis, which, we are told, "forms the foundation of all current speculations upon the subject;" or whether he will turn from these *reasonable explanations* for the existence of things, and take the plain, Word of truth, which says, "By the Word of the Lord were the heavens made;" "He spake and it was; he commanded and it stood fast," together with the explanation as given in Genesis and elsewhere in the Scriptures.

Faith and finite reason face each other; the education of the world takes reason; Christian education is based upon faith in God's Word. Which will develop character? *Why is it that modern science-study, does not lead to God?* In the evolutionary teaching of the nebular hypothesis you have one answer.

Picking up an ordinary text-book in zoology, we read: "The earliest member of the *series directly leading up to the horse* was eohippus, an older Eocene form about as large as a fox, which had four well-developed toes and the rudiments of a fifth on each forefoot, and three toes behind. In later Eocene beds appeared an animal of similar size, but with only four toes in front and three behind. In newer beds, i. e., lower Miocene, are found the remains of Mesohippus, which was as large as a sheep and had three toes and the splint of another in each forefoot....The succeeding forms were still more horse-like."[187] Next they find a donkey-like animal, and later "a true Equus, as large as the existing horse, appears just above the horizon, and the series is complete."[188]

If the horse tribe has evolved from a fox-like animal, it is little wonder that men trace their origin to the monkey tribe; but those who wish God's character, take by faith the statement that "in the image of God created He him."

Such theories form the basis for the generally adopted classification of the entire vegetable and animal worlds. Christian education demands new text- books, based upon the truths of God's Word. From Dana, the recognized authority on geology, the following sentences are quoted:

"Life commenced among plants, in *seaweeds*; and it ended in *palms, oaks, elms,* the *orange, rose,* etc. It commenced among animals in *lingulae* (mollusks standing on a stem like a plant), *crinoids, worms,* and *trilobites,* and probably earlier in the simple system-less protozoans; it ended in *man.*" For this development, he says, "Time is long."

In a paragraph on "Progress Always the Gradual Unfolding of a System," are the words: "There were higher and lower species appearing through *all the ages*, but the successive populations were still, in their general range, of higher and higher grade; and thus, the progress was ever upward. The type or plan of vegetation, and the four grand types or plans of animal life, the radiate, molluscan, articulate, and vertebrate, were each displayed under multitudes of tribes and species, *rising in rank with the progress of time....*Its progress should be, *as zoological history attests, a development, an unfolding, an evolution.*"

In the study of this evolution in animal life, he says, "The progress in the system of life is a progress in civilization," and he gives several illustrations, as the passage from tadpole to frog; from lobster to crab, from worm to insect, etc. Such teachers speak always of the evolution from the lower to the higher forms of life, but leave retrogression entirely out of their reckoning.

To those who offer the Sacred Record in opposition to his so-called geological proofs, Dana says: "The Biblical student finds, in the first chapter of Genesis, positive statement with regard to the creation of living beings. But these statements are often misunderstood; for they really leave the question as to the operation of natural causes for the most part an open one—as asserted by Augustine, among the fathers of the church and by some Biblical interpreters of the present day.

In view of the whole subject, the following appears to be the conclusions most likely to be sustained by further research: The evolution of the system of life went forward *through derivation of species from species, according to*

usual methods, not yet clearly understood, and with few occasions for supernatural intervention," etc.
Thus, have the truths in God's great lesson book of nature been misinterpreted. It was a step in the right direction when the mechanical drill of the classics was dropped, and nature studies substituted; but God's Word must take its place as the interpreter of nature and natural phenomena, or the theory of evolution is the natural result, and this will form no part of Christian education.

Protestant parents, are your children learning to see in the visible things about them the emblems of the Invisible, even the eternal Power and Godhead? If not, why do you not put them where they will? This is their salvation.

The exaltation of detail and the belittling of principles is a common error in educational systems. This is seen in all departments of learning. Not only is it exemplified in the exaltation of the mental and the physical above the spiritual, but the same method is employed in the detail work of the class room. This is in essence papal education. Christian education requires teachers to ever see the border throughout the whole course of instruction.

To illustrate the thought: There are a few fundamental principles which govern the universe. Such is the statement of the truth, "The love of Christ constraineth us," which contains within it the whole explanation of the force of gravity, adhesion, cohesion, molecular attraction, chemical affinity, human love, and the law of sex, and is therefore illustrated in physics, chemistry, mineralogy, biology—in fact, in all the sciences. Again, the second great commandment, "Thou shalt love thy neighbor as thyself," is the statement of a principle which underlies all history, civil government, and political and social science. If followed, it will solve all international difficulties, as well as prevent personal animosity; it will blot out the evils of society, breaking down the barrier between poverty and riches; trusts would never exist, trades unions would be unnecessary, and monopolies unknown, if the one law of Jehovah were only learned. Of how much greater value, then, is the study of such principles than all the theories which may be proposed by men for international arbitration, or all the laws which may be passed in legislative halls concerning the equal rights of men and the proper means of governing states, territories, or acquired possessions.

But this is Christian education, and lessons such as this are learned only when the truth is written on the heart by the pen of the Spirit. It is thus that a spiritual education, the higher birth of which the Saviour spoke, rises above the education of the world as far as heaven is above the earth. When these and kindred principles are made the central thought, all the facts which the pupil may be able to learn in a lifetime, will but serve to impress the truth more firmly on his life.

All the facts which it is possible for man to gather in a lifetime, added to all that are gathered by generation after generation, are but illustrations of a few principles. Modern teaching deals almost wholly with facts; it requires children, from the time they enter school until they are graduated, to heap together facts. Process is the great theme in mathematics; facts, facts, facts, are the things sought for in the whole realm of natural science. "History is but the study of still more facts, and where generalizations or classifications are made, they are theories formulated from the facts gathered. But man is never able to collect all the facts; he is never sure that his conclusions have reached absolute truth. The truth of the matter is, the classifications thus formed are only partially correct, and the discovery of a few more facts overthrows the fine-spun theories of the best of scientists. It is thus constantly in astronomy, in botany, in zoology, and in biology. Because of new discoveries, the physician of yesterday is wholly wrong in the eyes of the physician of today. Tomorrow the bright light of today will be superseded by some other luminary. This is the result of inductive reasoning based on sense perception.

This thought is well expressed by Hinsdale, who says: "We observe and register phenomena, classify facts, deduce conclusions and laws, and build up systems; but in science and philosophy we return to the subject again and again; we seek to verify our facts and test our conclusions, and when we have finished, we are not sure, save in a limited sphere, of our results. Some of the best-known sciences have been largely reorganized within the last few years. We have the 'new chemistry,' the 'new astronomy,' the 'new political economy,' and even the 'new mathematics.' Particularly in the field of human conduct, where man's, will is the governing faculty, we are often uncertain of our way and sometimes are wholly lost."[189]

The shifting foundation upon which such knowledge rests is well illustrated by the tests which the human being is able to make with the organs of sense. Water of 98° is hot to the hand that has been accustomed to a temperature of 45°, but cool to the hand which is just taken from water of 112°. An orange is sweet to the man who has been eating a stronger acid, but sour to the palate accustomed to sugar. The eye which has been used in a dimly lighted room is dazzled by the noonday glare, and judging of the size of a star by sight we would not conceive it to be a sun. The knowledge gained by the senses is only partially true—it is not absolute truth; and the scientific theories propounded by minds which have reasoned from these inaccurate data cannot fail to fall short of absolute truth. It may be *knowledge*; it is not *wisdom*.

Christian education approaches nature from the opposite direction. With a mind open to receive truth, it grasps *by faith* the statement of a universal principle. The spiritual law is the thing sought, and the corresponding physical law is compared with it. Once found, every fact which is learned, every observation made, but shows more clearly the working of that law in the spiritual world. For such teaching, faith is an indispensable attribute. Experiment is not discouraged, but strongly encouraged; reason is not laid aside, but the mind is called upon to reason on subjects grander and nobler than any deductions which can possibly result from the opposite manner of approaching truth.

This is the ideal in Christian education, the point toward which the Christian teacher is leading his pupils. In case of unbelief, or in dealing with the heathen, the mind must first be approached through the avenues of the senses, until the Spirit of God arouses the inner eye of faith. This is merely preliminary, and should not long continue. Children are not given credit for having the faith they really do possess, and are therefore held to the inductive method by educators long after their minds and hearts are capable of grasping truth, and when it would be found that the deductive method would produce a much more rapid growth of mental and spiritual power than is now seen.

This suggests the qualifications necessary on the part of a teacher. Remembering that this education is of a spiritual nature, the teacher himself must be connected with truth by an unwavering faith. When Nicodemus, the representative of higher education in the schools of Jerusalem, interviewed Christ, the new Teacher who had appeared in their midst, and whose teaching was attended by a power unknown to the educators of the day, the learned man said, "Rabbi, we know Thou art a teacher sent of God." "But *how* can these things be?" The heavenly Teacher outlined to him the secrets of His educational system, telling Nicodemus that it was not based on sight, but on faith; that the spiritual was first, and, when so made, the rest would follow. Then came the query, "How can it be?" To which Christ replied, "If I told you earthly things, and ye believe not, how shall ye believe if I tell you heavenly things?" "Art thou a master in Israel, and knowest not these things?"

In view of these thoughts, it is not strange that the study of the sciences in a Christian school will differ widely from the course offered in the same department of learning in an institution where the object of education is wholly different.

Discarding the evolutionary theory which pervades the teaching of all institutions where education is not wholly based on the Word of God, man, created in the image of God, is recognized as the highest manifestation of creative power. The life of God is the first study; that *life*, as manifested in man, is the next, and physiology takes its place as the center of all science-study. This is a study of life in all its manifestations, beginning with the spiritual, and extending to the mental and physical. Here, as elsewhere, the laws which govern the spiritual nature have their types in the other two natures; and when once the central truth of *life*, an abundance of life, is grasped, the study of physiology becomes not the study of dead forms, mere facts, but a soul-study, which includes the home of the inner man and all the machinery which the soul manipulates. Thus considered, from this center (physiology) extend rays, like the spokes of a wheel, each representing another science, until within that broad circle represented by these radii, are included all the physical as well as all the metaphysical sciences.

It will be seen that this mode of correlating the sciences cures at once the mistake of the age—the cramming system—which results from a neglect of manual training and from the study of a multiplicity of books, crowded with facts which must be stored in the mind of the student.

By placing physiology as the center of the circle, and correlating therewith all other sciences, another advantage arises, for that circle includes within itself the languages and mathematics. These latter are but helps in the study of the thought-bearing subjects—the Bible and the sciences— and instead of being studied as primary subjects, should be *used as a means to an end*. Reading, writing, spelling, grammar, rhetoric, and literature, and mathematics, from arithmetic to general geometry and calculus, are but means of expressing truths gained in the study of the revealed Word and the book of nature. The simplicity of the system will appeal to the mind of any educator, for it is a plan long sought for. The one thing lacking among those who have experimented with such methods has been the central subject, God's Word. Having truth as the basis for the correlation, the problem, so far as methods are concerned, is practically solved.

The great and pressing need is for teachers who can execute the plan. No narrow mind will be equal to the task. Again, as a system of true education is approached, is seen the exalted position to which those who teach are called.

Before passing the subject of physiology it is well to consider the meaning of the expression that this subject *"should be the basis of every educational effort."* Textbook study of physiology, it is clear, cannot cover this requirement. The fact is that *book-study* is but a small part of Christian education. True education is life, and he who learns much must live much. The food eaten, the manner of clothing the body, the study, exercise, mental habits, physical habits, manual training, in fact, every phase of life is a part of the study of physiology and hygiene, and these subjects must one and all receive due consideration by the Christian educator.

Manual training is becoming popular in many of our city schools, but the work offered in a Christian school will differ from that of the worldly school in this—the latter is training the hand or the eye only, the former is building character by giving a trade that enables the student to be self-supporting and independent. In that the aims are different, the methods must differ, although the matter taught may in many cases be identical.

Healthful living is receiving attention in many schools. The Christian school, while teaching the same subject, will have as its object a preparation for eternal life. The subject, taught without faith, will bring only increased physical and mental activity. The spiritual nature can be reached alone by that education which is based on faith.

Simply a casual investigation of the subject of Christian education reveals the need of books for the guidance of teachers who undertake to direct the growth of the child. With proper study-books, based upon the, eternal principles of truth revealed in the Scriptures, the work which is now in its infancy would make much more rapid and substantial progress.

Parents who sense the responsibility resting upon them in the rearing of children for the kingdom of heaven are anxious to know when and where the principles of Christian education can be carried out. The beauty of the system is nowhere more vividly portrayed than in the recognition which it gives to the *home* and the *duty of parents* toward their children in the matter of education.

In spite of the fact that much is said relative to the importance of educating for the state, the words of Herbert Spencer give a clear idea of the home as the center of the true system. He says: "As the family comes before the state in order of time—as the bringing up of children is possible before the state exists, or when it has ceased to be, whereas the state is rendered possible only by the bringing up of children, it follows that the duties of the parent demand closer attention than those of the citizen." The plan of Christian education goes a little farther, and recognizing the earthly family as a type of the heavenly, places the parents in God's place to the young children; hence the home should be the only school and "the parents should be the only teachers of their children until they have reached eight or ten years of age."

"The mother should find time to cultivate in herself and in her children a love for the beautiful buds and opening flowers....The only schoolroom for children from eight to ten years of age should be in the open air, amid the opening flowers and nature's beautiful scenery. And their only text-book should be the treasures of nature."

With such a training, the first ten years the child should develop a strong body and a strong mind. He should then be able to spend the next five or six years under the instruction of a consecrated Christian teacher in an elementary school, where teacher and parents may co-operate. The threefold nature must be developed so that when the age of manhood or womanhood is reached, strength of character has also been gained.

The youth should then continue, his mental culture in some industrial school, located in the country, where there is freedom from the evils of city life, and where the rapidly developing physical nature can be correctly guided into lines of practical duties which will fit him for real life. In the, meantime, mental culture and spiritual training are continued, for character is being formed for eternity.

The young man or woman of twenty or twenty-two should be prepared to select a life-work, and the special training needed can be received in a training school, which in Christian education will be for Christian workers. Such a school will be necessary; for the education thus outlined, extending from infancy over twenty years, cannot fail to develop a character which chooses *Christian work* as the life occupation. A short training in a higher institution, which in character is *a school of the prophets*, should so round out the nature already forming that the young person goes out an ambassador for Christ, willing to be used in any capacity by the Commander of the heavenly host, whether it be on the farm, at the carpenter's bench, or in the pulpit; for his soul is knit to the King of heaven, as was David's to Jonathan's. Such a student is prepared for active service, either on earth or in the kingdom of our God; for he is one with the Father and his Son.

"Comenius divided the first twenty-four years of life into four periods, to each of which he would assign a special school, thus:—

1. For infancy, the school should be the mother's knee.

2. For childhood the school should be the vernacular school.

3. For boyhood, the Latin school or gymnasium.

4. For youth, the university and travel.

"A mother should exist in every house, a vernacular school in every hamlet and village, a gymnasium in every city, and a university in every kingdom or in every province....The mother and the vernacular school embrace all the young of both sexes. The Latin school gives a more thorough education to those who aspire higher than the workshop; while the university trains up the teachers and the learned men of the future, that our churches, schools, and states may never lack suitable leaders."

In the system known as Christian education the division is about the same, the years of student life extending perhaps to thirty instead of twenty-four, with this division: the first ten years are spent in the home school; from ten to fifteen in the church school; from fifteen to twenty in the industrial school, and the years from twenty to twenty-five or even thirty are devoted to study and active work in the training school for workers.

The time now is when those who are true Protestants *will* demand Christian education, and when no sacrifice will be considered too great for the accomplishment of that object. The prophecy of Zechariah, recorded in the ninth chapter, gives the words of God concerning the contest to take place near the close of time between the sons of Greece and the sons of Zion. "Turn you to the stronghold, ye prisoners of hope; even today do I declare that I will render double unto thee; when I have bent Judah for Me, filled the bow with Ephraim, and raised up thy sons, O Zion, against thy sons, O Greece."

Greece is recognized in the Scriptures as emblematic of worldly wisdom,[190] but by that wisdom the world knew not God; in fact, by that wisdom the world was led away from God. God will, then, raise up the sons of Zion, the representatives of His wisdom—the divine philosophy—against the sons of Greece, or the students of the wisdom of the world; and in the final conflict, when truth wins, it will be evident that those who are numbered with the victors have forsaken the wisdom of Greece for the wisdom of God. It is not theory, but the most solemn fact, that the preparation for a life with God demands that we and our children receive a far different education than has been offered in the past. If we wish the highest culture, if we long for soul development, our education must be spiritual in nature; we must leave the low, turbid waters of the valley for the snow waters of Lebanon. This is Christian education.

Protestants today see their children slipping from the fold. Every inducement in the way of entertainments, form, ceremony, and oratory is used to attract the youth to the church, but still the world allures them. Ministers are beginning to search for the reason, and are attributing it to the character of the education now given in our schools; in saying this, they strike at the root of the trouble. Protestantism is dying; the form of godliness, which denies the power thereof, is spreading its dark mantle over the earth. It is in vain that we point to stately edifices or noted divines; if we cannot recognize the difficulty, it but proves that we are ourselves under the cloud, and recovery is all but impossible.

We talk of the spread of Christianity; we give of our means for the conversion of the heathen, while our children perish within our very homes. The spirit and power of Elias, which was to accompany the preaching of the kingdom of Christ, was "to turn the hearts of the fathers to the children," Cries the prophet Joel, "*Gather the children*, and those that suck the breast....Let the priests, the ministers of the Lord, weep between the porch and the altar, and let them say, Spare Thy people, O Lord, and give not Thine heritage [the children] to reproach, that the heathen should rule over them."

Ministers, fathers, mothers, look to the welfare of your children, or the cause of Protestantism is lost in America. Take up your first, your all-important duty, and give your children a Christian education, and instead of a decline in church membership as now reported, there will be an increase; instead of formalism, there will be life. This will be the means of bringing the heathen to your door, and to a knowledge of the gospel.

"Lift up thine eyes round about, and behold; all these gather themselves together, and come to thee. As I live, saith the Lord, thou shalt surely clothe thee with them all, as with an ornament, and bind them on thee, as a bride doeth. For thy waste and thy desolate places and the land of thy destruction, shall even now be too narrow by reason of the inhabitants....*The children which thou shalt have, after thou hast lost the other,* shall say again in thine ears, the place is too strait for me; give place to me that I may dwell. Then shalt thou say in thine heart, Who hath begotten me these, seeing I have lost my children, and am desolate?... Who hath brought up these? Behold, I was left alone; these, where had they been? Thus saith the Lord God, Behold! I will lift up Mine hand to the Gentiles, and set up My standard to the people; and they shall bring thy sons in their arms, and thy daughters shall be carried upon their shoulders. And kings shall be thy nursing fathers, and their queens thy nursing mothers; they shall bow down to thee with their faces toward the earth, and lick up the dust of thy feet....For I will contend with him that contendeth with thee, *and I will save thy children.*"[191]

How will He save the children? "All thy children shall be taught of the Lord." When will the Gentiles come bringing their children to supply the places of those now lost? When Protestants can show to the Gentiles that they have a system of education which is free from the errors now so prevalent; when they can teach the Gentiles the truth.

"Sing, O barren, thou that didst not bear; break forth into singing, and cry aloud, thou that didst not travail with child: for more are the children of the desolate than the children of the married wife, saith the Lord. Enlarge the place of thy tent, and let them stretch forth the curtains of thine habitations: spare not, lengthen thy cords, and strengthen thy stakes; for thou shalt break forth on the right hand and on the left; and thy seed shall inherit the Gentiles."[192]

When shall these things be? The same chapter of Isaiah answers. When "all thy children shall be taught of the

Lord." When Protestants educate according to the principles of true Protestantism, then will the words of the same prophet, recorded in the sixtieth chapter, be fulfilled. "Arise, be enlightened, for thy light cometh....The Gentiles shall come to thy light and kings to the brightness of thy rising....Thy sons shall come from far, and thy daughters shall be nursed at thy side."[193]

Christ came, fulfilling in every particular the prophecies quoted. "As thou hast sent Me into the world, even so have I also sent them into the world," are the words of Christ to His church. As Christ was a teacher, so that church which does the work which the Christian church *must* do, will have a system of education, and its members will be educators indeed.

Of Christ as a teacher it is written, "He raised Himself above all others whom millions today regard as their grandest teachers. Buddha, Confucius, Mohammed, to say nothing of Greek and Roman sages, are not worthy to be compared with Christ." Says Paroz: "Jesus Christ, in founding a new religion, has laid the foundation of a new education in the bosom of humanity."

"In lowliness and humility," writes Dr. Schaff, "in the form of a servant as to the flesh, yet effulgent with divine glory, the Saviour came forth from a despised corner of the earth; destroyed the power of evil in our nature; realized in His spotless life, and in His sufferings, the highest idea of virtue and piety, lifted the world with His pierced hands out of its distress; reconciled men to God, and gave a new direction to the whole current of history."

It is the education which He taught, which was His very life even in the courts of heaven, which Protestants are now entreated to accept. "Today if ye will hear His voice, harden not your hearts."

Where are the Protestants who are true to the name? Where are the schools which will teach the things of God? Where are the teachers who forsake secular methods, as did the Reformers, to become teachers for Christ?

Earth with its inhabitants is to the heart of God the most precious part of the creation. As a recreant child draws harder on the parent's sympathy, so the world, because of the sinfulness of sin, has brought heaven and earth in touch. The universe sees streaming from the throne rays of light and love, pointing to the one spot in all creation where sin abounds. They tell the story of the cross. The perfect harmony which forms the "music of the spheres," which was marred when man fell, will again pervade all space when the plan of salvation is complete, and our earth again joins in the great chorus of the sons of God.

For six thousand years creation has groaned, waiting for our redemption. The completion of the plan draws nigh, and for the final struggle everything is now assuming an intensity never before seen. Principles of truth, for centuries hidden, or known only in part, will again shine forth in their original splendor. The wisdom of the ages will be manifest in the closing era of the world's history. True, this wisdom will often appear but "foolishness" in the eyes of those who oppose truth; but spiritual things are spiritually discerned, and the Spirit of the Holy One will once more brood over the whole earth, taking up its abode in those hearts which beat in unison with the strains of heaven. Christian education binds earth to heaven. The wise in heart will return to the God-given system of education, choosing "the fountains of living waters" instead of hewing "them out cisterns, that can hold no water."[194]

Authorities Referred to or Quoted In This Book

BUCKLEY, editor of *Christian Advocate*.
BOONE, "Education in the United States."
BOK, editor of *Ladies' Home Journal*.
D'AUBIGNÉ, "History of the Reformation."
DANA, "Geology."
DRAPER, "Intellectual Development of Europe."
DABNEY, president of the University of Tennessee.
EMERSON, "Representative Men."
FISKE, "Beginnings of New England."
FENTON, "Epistles of Paul."
GIBBON, "Decline and Fall of the Roman Empire."
HINSDALE, "Jesus as a Teacher."
HARRIS, U. S. Commissioner of Education.
HARPER, president of Chicago University.
HARTMAN, "Religion or No Religion in Education."
KAREL, U. S. Consul-General to Russia.
LAURIE, "Rise and Constitution of Universities."
MOSHEIM, "Church History."
MESCHERSKI, of the Department of Agriculture of Russia.
NEANDER, "Church History."
PAINTER, "History of Education."
RANKE, "History of the Popes."
ROSENKRANZ, "Philosophy of Education."
STUMP, "Life of Melanchthon."
THOMPSON, "Footprints of the Jesuits."

Footnotes

1. Job 28.
2. I Cor. 2:6, R. V., mar.
3. Ps. 33:9.
4. Eze. 28:12-14.
5. Eze. 28:14, 17.
6. Isa. 14:13, 14.
7. Ps. 33:9.
8. Gen. 1:2, R. V.
9. Gen. 1:20, R. V., mar.
10. Gen. 21:26-8.
11. Gen. 2:17.
12. Rev. 2:7.
13. 2 Peter 3:5-7.
14. Luke 17:26.
15. Heb. 11:8-10; Rom. 4:20.
16. Gen. 15:23.
17. Gal. 4:22, 25.
18. Deut. 4:5, 6.
19. "History of Education," page 29.
20. "Jesus as a Teacher," pages 28-30.
21. "Jesus as a Teacher," page 31.
22. "History of Education," page 28.
23. "Jesus as a Teacher," page 30.
24. "Jesus as a Teacher," page 31.
25. "History of Education," page 29.
26. "History of Education," page 27.
27. Deuteronomy 28.
28. Proverbs 31.
29. See 2 Chron. 17:6-13.
30. Daniel 10.
31. Deut. 4:20. 2
32. Matt. 2:15.
33. Rom. 1:18-20, Fenton's translation.
34. Idem. verses 21-25.
35. I Cor. 1:18-26, Fenton's translation.
36. "History of Education," pages 32, 34.
37. "History of Education," page 65.
38. Emerson, "Representative Men."
39. 1 Cor. 2:1-5, Fenton's trans.
40. Col. 2:8.
41. Heb. 11:13.
42. Isa. 11:12.
43. "History of Education," page 121.
44. Heb. 11:3.
45. 2 Kings 17:15-17; Jer. 19:4, 5.
46. See John 1:14, R. V., mar.
47. Prov. 22:6.
48. John 3.
49. "Jesus as a Teacher," pages 48, 49.
50. John 4.
51. "Jesus as a Teacher," page 72.
52. Rev. 1:10.
53. History of Education," page 84.
54. John 16:29, 30.
55. John 17:15-17.
56. Rev. 2:2, 3.
57. Rev 6:2
58. "History of Education," page 90.
59. Church History, cent. 1, part 2 chap. 3, sec. 7
60. 2 Tim. 2:2.
61. Idem.
62. "Decline and Fall of the Roman Empire," chap. 23, par. 21.
63. "Church History," cent. 2, part 2, chap. 1, par. 6.
64. Rev. 2:4, 5.
65. 1 Cor. 2:3-5, 13, Fenton's translation.
66. "Church History," cent. 3, part 1, chap. 1, par. 5.
67. "Church History," Torrey's trans, vol. 1, pages 71, 73.
68. "Church History," Maclain's trans., cent. 1, part 2, chap. 3, par. 10.
69. Idem.
70 See Torrey's trans., vol. 2, page 237.
71. "Church History," vol. 2, pages 224, 225.
72. Idem, page 226.
73. Idem, page 238.
74. Idem, page 242.
75. See Chambers's Encyclopedia.

76. Quoted by Neander, "Church History," vol. 2, pp. 463, 464.
77. Rev. 13:1.
78. "Church History," Maclain's trans., cent. 3, chap. 3, par. 1.
79. Idem, Murdock's trans., cent. 3, part 2, chap. 3, par. 5.
80. Mosheim, "Church History," Maclain's trans., cent. 3, chap. 3, par. 2.
81. "Intellectual Development of Europe," vol. 1, page 432, 434.
82. "History of the Reformation," book 1, chap. 1.
83. "Rise and Constitution of Universities," page 55.
84. Idem, page 56.
85. W.T. Harris, U.S. Commissioner of Education.
86. Idem.
87. "Intellectual Development of Europe," vol. 2, page 191.
88. "Church History," cent. 11, part 2, chap. 1, sec. 5.
89. "History of Education," page 100.
90. "Church History," cent. 11, part 2, chap. 1, sec. 5.
*91. "Intellectual Development of Europe," vol. 2, page 159.
92. "Intellectual Development of Europe," vol. 2, page 121.
93. Idem.
94. Idem.
95. Idem, page 125.
96. Idem, pages 125, 126.
97. "Church History," cent. 12, part 2, chap. 1, par. 4.
98. "History of Education," page 114
99. Idem.
100. Laurie, "Rise and Constitution of Universities," page 168.
101. Idem, pages 219, 220.
102. Idem, page 169.
103. Idem, page 222
104. Idem, page 227.
105. Idem, page 220.
106. Rev. B. Hartman, "Religion or No Religion in Education," page 43.
107. "History of Education," pages 115, 116.
108. (See "Students in Riot," at the Chicago University, Chicago Record, Dec. 2, 1899.
109. "Rise and Constitution of Universities," page 288.
110. "History of Education," page 119.
111. Idem, page 121.
112. "History of Education," pages 125-128.
113. "History of Education," page 138.
114. Idem, pages 139, 140.
115. "History of Education," pages 142, 143.
116. "History of the Reformation," book 10, chap. 9.
117. Ibid.
118. Ibid.
119. "History of Education," page 143.
120. Idem.
121. D'Aubigné, book 10, chap. 9.
122. Quoted in "History of Education," page 145.
123. "History of Education," page 149.
124. Idem, page 135.
125. "History of the Reformation," book 4, chap. 3.
126. "History of the Reformation," book 4, chap. 3.
127. "Life of Melanchthon," page 81.
128. "History of the Reformation," book 3. chap. 9.
129. "History of the Popes," Kelley's trans., book 5, pages 132-135.
130. Idem, page 134.
131. "History of Education," page 155.
132. Idem.
133. "History of Education," pages 154, 155.
134. Idem.
135. Idem, page 156.
136. "History of Education," page 160.
137. Idem, page 162.
138. Idem, page 163.
139. "Philosophy of Education," page 267.

140. "History of Education," pages 165, 166.
141. "Philosophy of Education," page 270.
142. Idem, pages 271, 272.
143. "History of Education," pages 171, 172.
144. Idem, pages 172, 173.
145. "History of the Popes," book 5, pages 134, 137-139.
146. Idem, page 146.
147. "Footprints of the Jesuits," page 133.
148. "History of the Popes," book 5, page 152.
149. Idem, page 252.
150. Fiske, "United States History," page 54.
151. "Papacy and Civil Powers," page 685.
152. Idem, page 98.
153. "Footprints of the Jesuits," page 419.
154. Idem, page 408.
155. Boone, "Education in the United States," page 8.
156. "Beginnings of New England," pages 62, 63.
157. E. E. White, "Proceedings of National Educational Association," 1882.
158. Idem, page 66.
159. "Beginnings of New England," page 146.
160. "Education in the United States," page 30.
161. Idem, page 20.
162. "Education in the United States," pages 23, 24, 29.
163. Idem, page 25.
164. "Education in the United States," pages 76, 77.
165. "Education in the United States" page 104.
166. "Education in the United States," pages 158, 159.
167. Ladies' Home Journal, January, 1900.
168. The Christian Advocate, February, 1900.
169. "Education in the United States," page 190.
170. Idem.
171. "Education in the United States," pages 267, 268.
172. "History of Education," page 173.
173. Quoted by Painters "History of Education," page 191.
174. "The Murder of the Modern Innocents," Ladies' Home Journal, February, 1900.
175. North American Review, April, 1900,
176. "Encyclopedia Britannica," Art. Socrates.
177. Outlook, April 21, 1900.
178. Literary Digest, May 26, 1900.
179. Report for 1896-97, vol. l, Introduction.
180. Report of the Commissioner of Education, 1896-97, vol. I, page 369.
181. "History of Education," page 217.
182. See Cosmopolitan, February, 1900.
183. Arena, October, 1894.
184. Report of Commissioner of Education, 1897-98, vol. 2, pages 1632, 1633.
185. "History of Education," page 1.
186. Idem, page 274.
187. Packard's "Brief Course," page 277, (published by Henry Holt & Co.) of New York.
188. Marsh.
189. "Jesus as a Teacher," page 48.
190. I Corinthians 1.
191. Isa. 49:18-25.
192. Isa. 54:1-3.
193. Isa. 60:1-4, mar.
194. Jer. 2:13.

Made in the USA
Monee, IL
13 May 2023

33321021R00134